SNIPES

D1536363

WOE OR WONDER

The Emotional Effect
of Shakespearean Tragedy

J. V. Cunningham

THE **SWALLOW PRESS** INC.
CHICAGO

WOE OR WONDER first published by the
University of Denver Press, copyright 1951
by J. V. Cunningham.

Reprinted as part of
TRADITION AND POETIC STRUCTURE

Alan Swallow, 1960

Swallow Paperbooks edition, 1964

Second printing, 1969

TO THE MEMORY OF W. D. BRIGGS

Contents

Introduction:
Ripeness is All

I am concerned in these essays with understanding precisely what Shakespeare meant. It is true that "when we read Shakespeare's plays," as one scholar says, "we are always meeting our own experiences and are constantly surprised by some phrase which expresses what we thought to be our own secret or our own discovery."[1] But the danger is that the meaning we find may really be our own secret, our own discovery, rather than Shakespeare's, and the more precious and beguiling for being our own. The danger I have in mind can be illustrated by our attitude toward one of the most famous of Shakespearean phrases, "Ripeness is all." It is a favorite quotation of Mr. Eliot's. "It seems to me," he says in discussing the question of truth and belief in poetry, "to have profound emotional meaning, with, at least, no literal fallacy."[2] He does not specify what this meaning is, but I take it that it is something not strictly denotative though emotionally compelling.

The phrase, indeed, has seemed to many to represent a profound intuition into reality and to sum up the essence of Shakespearean, or even of human, tragedy. It speaks quite nearly to us. What it means to each will perhaps depend on his own experience and his own way of relating the texture of experience to the insights of literature. Yet all would agree that "Ripeness is all" gathers into a phrase something of the ultimate value of this life; it reassures us that maturity of experience is a final good, and that there is a fulness of feeling, an inner and emotional completion in life that is attainable and that will resolve our tragedies. Such at least seems to be the interpretation of a recent critic. "After repeated disaster," he says of Gloucester in *King Lear:*

he can assent, "And that's true too," to Edgar's "Ripeness is all." For man may ripen into fulness of being, which means, among other things, that one part of him does not rule all the rest and that one moment's mood does not close off all the perspectives available to him.[3]

In this way we discover in Shakespeare's phrase the secret morality of our own times. It is a meaning I can enter into quite as deeply as anyone, but it is not what Shakespeare meant.

Shakespeare meant something much more traditional. The phrase occurs in *King Lear*. In an earlier scene Edgar had prevented Gloucester from committing suicide, that act which consummates the sin of despair, and Gloucester had accepted the situation in the true spirit of Christian resignation:

> henceforth I'll bear
> Affliction till it do cry out itself
> 'Enough, enough,' and die.
> 4. 6. 75-7

But now Gloucester seems to relapse for a moment, saying:

> No further, sir; a man may rot even here.

And Edgar stiffens his resolution with these words:

> Men must endure
> Their going hence even as their coming hither:
> Ripeness is all.
> 5. 2. 9-11

The context is the desire for death. The conclusion is that as we were passive to the hour of our birth so we must be passive to the hour of our death. So far, surely, the speech is an affirmation of the spirit of resignation, and it would be reasonable to suppose that the summary clause at the end, "Ripeness is all," is but the final restatement of this attitude. It was certainly an available attitude. The experience of Christian resignation was dense with the history of the Western spirit, and that history was alive and present in Shakespeare's time; it spoke daily from the pulpit and in the private consolations of

8

intimate friends. The theme, furthermore, was a favorite with Shakespeare. It had been fully explored in the Duke's great speech in *Measure for Measure*:

> Be absolute for death. Either death or life
> Will thereby be the sweeter. Reason thus with life:
> If I do lose thee I do lose a thing
> That none but fools would keep. A breath thou art,
> Servile to all the skyey influences
> That do this habitation where thou keep'st
> Hourly afflict. Merely thou art death's fool;
> For him thou labour'st by thy flight to shun,
> And yet runn'st toward him still. . .
>   Yet in this life
> Lie hid moe thousand deaths; yet death we fear
> That makes these odds all even.
>   3. 1. 5-13, 39-41

But the finest expression, other than in the passage from *Lear*, is Hamlet's speech to Horatio as he goes to the catastrophe:

> . . . we defy augury; there's a special providence in the fall of a sparrow. If it be now, 'tis not to come; if it be not to come, it will be now; if it be not now, yet it will come: the readiness is all.   5. 2. 230-3

This is as much as to say that we must endure our going hence, be it when it may, since the hour of our death is in the care of Providence: *the readiness is all.*

It has been said that this is Stoic, and certainly *augury* hints toward Antiquity. But he who speaks of a special providence in the fall of a sparrow could trust an audience in the age of Elizabeth to think of Christian theology and the New Testament:

> And fear not them which kill the body, but are not able to kill the soul: but rather fear him which is able to destroy both body and soul in hell. Are not two sparrows sold for a farthing? *and one of them shall not fall on the ground without your Father.* But the very hairs of your head are all numbered. Fear ye not therefore, ye are of more value than many sparrows.

Watch therefore: for ye know not what hour your Lord doth come. But know this, that if the goodman of the house had known in what watch the thief would come, he would have watched, and would not have suffered his house to be broken up. *Therefore be ye also ready*: for in such hour as ye think not the Son of man cometh.

It was not only Seneca and his sons who could urge men to meet death with equanimity. Bishop Latimer, the Protestant martyr, in a sermon preached before King Edward VI speaks the thought and almost the words of Hamlet:

Unusquisque enim certum tempus habet praedefinitum a Domino: "For every man hath a certain time appointed him of God, and God hideth that same time from us." For some die in young age, some in old age, according as it pleaseth him. He hath not manifested to us the time because he would have us at all times ready; else if I knew the time, I would presume upon it, and so should be worse. But he would have us ready at all times, and therefore he hideth the time of our death from us. . . . But of that we may be sure, there shall not fall one hair from our head without his will; and we shall not die before the time that God hath appointed unto us: which is a comfortable thing, specially in time of sickness or wars. . . . There be some which say, when their friends are slain in battle, "Oh, if he had tarried at home, he should not have lost his life." These sayings are naught: for God hath appointed every man his time. To go to war in presumptuousness, without an ordinary calling, such going to war I allow not: but when thou art called, go in the name of the Lord; and be well assured in thy heart that thou canst not shorten thy life with well-doing.[4]

The similarity of the phrase in *Hamlet* to the one in *Lear* is so close that the first may be taken as the model and prototype of the other. But in *Lear* the phrase has been transmuted, and with it the idea and attitude. The deliberate and developed rhetoric of *Measure for Measure* has served its purpose to explore the area of experience, and has been put aside. The riddling logicality of Hamlet's speech has been simplified to the bare utterance of:

> Men must endure
> Their going hence even as their coming hither

and the concept of the arbitrariness of birth has been introduced to reinforce the arbitrariness of death. Finally, Hamlet's precise and traditional statement, "the readiness is all," has been transformed into a metaphor.

What does the metaphor mean? There is no need for conjecture; it had already by the time of *Lear* become trite with use, and with use in contexts closely related to this. In Thomas Wilson's *Art of Rhetoric* (1560) we read:

> Among fruit we see some apples are soon ripe and fall from the tree in the midst of summer; other be still green and tarry till winter, and hereupon are commonly called winter fruit: even so it is with man, some die young, some die old, and some die in their middle age.[5]

Shakespeare has Richard in *Richard II* comment on the death of John of Gaunt:

> The ripest fruit first falls, and so doth he:
> His time is spent . . .
>
> 2. 1. 153-4

That is, as fruit falls in the order of ripeness, so a man dies when his time is spent, at his due moment in the cosmic process. Again, Touchstone's dry summary of life and time in *As You Like It*:

> And so, from hour to hour, we ripe and ripe,
> And then, from hour to hour, we rot and rot . . .
>
> 2. 7. 26-7

does not mean that we ripen to maturity and then decline, but that we ripen toward death, and then quite simply and with no metaphors rot.

But death is not incidental to Shakespearean tragedy; it is rather the defining characteristic. Just as a Shakespearean comedy is a play that has a clown or two and ends in marriages, so a tragedy involves characters of high estate and concludes with violent deaths. The principle of its being is death, and when this is achieved the play is ended. In this sense, then, "Ripeness is all" is the structural principle of Shakespearean tragedy. Thus in *Richard III* the Cassandra-like chorus, the old Queen Margaret, enters alone as the play draws rapidly on to the final catastrophe and says:

> So now prosperity begins to mellow
> And drop into the rotten mouth of death
> > 4. 4. 1-2

And in *Macbeth,* Malcolm says toward the close:

> Macbeth
> Is ripe for shaking, and the pow'rs above
> Put on their instruments.
> > 4. 3. 237-9

In this passage the powers above, who are the agents of Providence, are associated with the ripened time. Providence is destiny, and in tragedy destiny is death.

By "Ripeness is all," then, Shakespeare means that the fruit will fall in its time, and man dies when God is ready. The phrase gathers into the simplest of sentences, the most final of linguistic patterns, a whole history of attempted formulations, and by the rhetorical device of a traditional metaphor transposes a state into a process. Furthermore, the metaphor shifts our point of view from a man's attitude toward death, from the "readiness" of Hamlet and the "Men must endure" of the first part of Edgar's speech, to the absoluteness of the external process of Providence on which the attitude depends.

But this is not what the phrase means to the uninstructed modern reader, and this poses a problem. The modern meaning is one that is dear to us and one that is rich and important in itself. It would be natural to ask, Need we give it up? I see

12

no reason why we should give up the meaning: maturity of experience is certainly a good, and the phrase in a modern context is well enough fitted to convey this meaning. But it is our phrase now, and not Shakespeare's, and we should accept the responsibility for it. The difference in meaning is unmistakable: ours looks toward life and his toward death; ours finds its locus in modern psychology and his in Christian theology. If we are secure in our own feelings we will accept our own meanings as ours, and if we have any respect for the great we will penetrate and embrace Shakespeare's meaning as his. For our purpose in the study of literature, and particularly in the historical interpretation of texts, is not in the ordinary sense to further the understanding of ourselves. It is rather to enable us to see how we could think and feel otherwise than as we do. It is to erect a larger context of experience within which we may define and understand our own by attending to the disparity between it and the experience of others.

In fact, the problem that is here raised with respect to literature is really the problem of any human relationship: Shall we understand another on his terms or on ours? It is the problem of affection and truth, of appreciation and scholarship. Shakespeare has always been an object of affection and an object of study. Now, it is common experience that affection begins in misunderstanding. We see our own meanings in what we love and we misconstrue for our own purposes. But life will not leave us there, and not only because of external pressures. What concerns us is naturally an object of study. We sit across the room and trace the lineaments of experience on the face of concern, and we find it is not what we thought it was. We come to see that what Shakespeare is saying is not what we thought he was saying, and we come finally to appreciate it for what it is. Where before we had constructed the fact from our feeling, we now construct our feeling from the fact. The end of affection and concern is accuracy and truth, with an alteration but no dimunition of feeling.

II

Aught of Woe or Wonder

Whatever emotion and whatever tragedy may be, it has always been said that tragedy, and especially the tragic catastrophe, evokes strong and specific emotions. The doctrine is common to Antiquity and the present day as well as to Shakespeare and the Renaissance. "In undertaking any piece of literature," Erasmus remarks in a little Renaissance treatise on how to teach, "it is advisable to show what kind of work it is, the nature of its subject-matter, and what especially is to be looked for in that kind of work. . . . In tragedy one looks especially for the emotional effects, which are quite strong, and then for the means by which these effects are excited."[1] The nature of the effects, however, alters from period to period as the nature of tragedy alters and as the quality and structure of the emotional life varies from society to society, for there is a history of the emotions as well as a history of ideas. The effects we are concerned with here are those of Shakespearean tragedy and those specifically intended by the author and supported by his tradition. The question is, What emotional effects did Shakespeare intend to be evoked by the catastrophe of his greater tragedies?

I

We are told explicitly at the end of *Hamlet* what the emotional effect of the tragic catastrophe is: it is one of fear, sorrow, and wonder. The point is made in two passages, the first of which reads:

I follow thee.
I am dead, Horatio. Wretched queen, adieu!
You that look pale and tremble at this chance,
That are but mutes or audience to this act,
Had I but time (as this fell sergeant, Death,
Is strict in his arrest) O, I could tell you—
But let it be. Horatio, I am dead;
Thou liv'st; report me and my cause aright
To the unsatisfied.

5. 2. 343-51

The scene is familiar to every reader: the King and Queen are dead, Laertes has uttered his last words. And now Hamlet, in a fashion conventional to the Elizabethan drama, addresses his remarks rapidly to one character after another—to the dying Laertes, to Horatio, to the Queen; and finally he turns to the other actors on the stage, to the "mutes" who serve as "audience to this act." These "look pale and tremble": it is their function to express the proper emotional attitude and so to convey that attitude directly to the larger audience who witness the play, for emotional effects are directly transferrable; indeed, they are much more communicable than ideas.

The way in which this process was understood in Shakespeare's time is explained by his contemporary, Thomas Dekker, in the prologue to one of his plays:

That man give me whose breast filled by the Muses
With rapture into a second them infuses;
Can give the actor sorrow, rage, joy, passion,
Whilst he again by self-same agitation
Commands the hearers, sometimes drawing out tears,
Then smiles, and fills them both with hopes and fears.[2]

The dramatist derives emotions from his sources of inspiration, infuses them into the actor, who in turn communicates them to the audience. The scheme of thought here is Platonic. It is that which Socrates explains to the professional reciter of Homer in Plato's dialogue *Ion* under the figure of a magnetic chain of attraction (533C), and doubtless is borrowed from that model. The Muse inspires Homer as a magnet moves an iron ring, the reciter Ion is moved by Homer as another ring by the magnetized one, and the audience finally is moved by Ion, so that three rings hang like a chain from the magnet. Thus feeling runs directly from the sources of poetry to the audience through the medium of poet and actor, and the emotions which in this case Ion excites in his hearers—fear, sorrow, and wonder (535B-C)[3]—are curiously enough those which Shakespeare in *Hamlet* ascribes to the tragic catastrophe. They are also, of course, the emotional effects which Aristotle ascribes to Greek tragedy—pity and fear, certainly, and as we shall see, wonder, too.[4]

The particular emotion denominated in the first passage from *Hamlet* is the conventional tragic effect of fear or terror, for to "look pale and tremble" are the very marks and signs of this. Richard in *Richard III* queries Buckingham on his qualifications for the role of tragic villain:

Come, cousin, can'st thou quake and change thy color . . .
    As if thou wert distraught and mad with terror?
And Buckingham reassures him:
    TUT. I can counterfeit the deep tragedian . . .
                                    3. 5. 1, 4-5

The emotion of fear is evoked by "this chance," in men who are "mutes or audience to this act." What is the precise meaning of "this act" and "this chance," since it is with respect to these that the effect is predicated? *Act* in such contexts signifies the particular course of events under consideration. So the First Gentleman comments on the narration of those extraordinary events that untangle the knot of the *Winter's Tale:* "The dignity of this act was worth the audience of kings and princes, for by such was it acted" (5. 2. 86-8). And Prospero in the *Tempest,* referring to the whole business of his deposition and exile, says to Alonso: "Thy brother was a furtherer in this act"

(5. 1. 73). But the closest parallel to the present passage is in the final speech in *Othello* where Lodovico, the representative of the Venetian state, closes the play thus:

> Myself will straight aboard, and to the state
> This heavy act with heavy heart relate.

This heavy act—that is, "The tragic loading of this bed," the deaths of Desdemona and Othello. There is here an exact correspondence between the quality of the events and the quality of the emotion they evoke, between the heaviness of act and the heaviness of heart. Similarly the emotion of fear or terror would naturally be provoked by such fearful and terrible events as the deaths of the King, Queen, and Laertes, and the imminent death of Hamlet himself.

"This chance" has a meaning similar to "this act." It is, furthermore, a notion and a term intimately associated with the central Elizabethan conception of tragedy, and especially of the tragic catastrophe. It concentrates in a word the two main aspects of that event, aspects that had long been fused in the Latin equivalent, *casus*. For that word may signify, as it does in the late medieval collections of tragic stories, the fall and death of a great figure which constitutes the catastrophe; and it may also signify the external cause of such a fall, the operation of that agency which to man seems Chance or Fortune, but which from a true and theological point of view is to be regarded as the unfolding of Divine Providence. Indeed, nothing really happens by Chance or Fortune with respect to an absolute God, but only with respect to secondary causes: *nihil est a casu vel fortuna respectu Dei, sed respectu ceterarum causarum.*[5] Hence the display on the stage of the operation of Chance, which is but the inscrutable ways of Divine Providence, strikes the witnesses with fear and terror when the case is notable, for it illuminates the disparity between the relative world of man and the absoluteness of the Eternal Cause.

The bare word, of course, though shot through with the

larger meanings of that historic term, does not carry with it such a full and explicit theory as has just been sketched. Yet its use here does imply the prior existence of such a context. What the bare word means can be ascertained by glancing through a Shakespeare concordance: the meaning ranges from the relatively colorless significance of "ordinary happening or event," through the denomination of such events as make up a narrative (*Cymb* 5. 5. 391), to the strictly philosophical significance of "Chance or Fortune." But the phrase, "this chance," has also a special and restricted meaning. It means the fall and death of notable persons and has in it an element of suddenness and surprise, of the apparently fortuitous.

For example, in the *Tragedy of Locrine* (about 1591), a bad but representative play, the chorus promises us:

> the sequel shall declare
> What tragic chances fall out in this war.
>
> 2 Prol., 16-7[6]

And fall they do, one after another. So also King Henry in *3 Henry VI* speaks of the dead slain in battle:

> How will the country for these woful chances
> Misthink the king, and not be satisfied!
>
> 2. 5. 107-8

But the best example is in *Macbeth*, where Macbeth speaks of the murder of Duncan after its accomplishment:

> Had I but died an hour before this chance,
> I had liv'd a blessed time.
>
> 2. 3. 96-7

That is, "My life had ended in the state of grace *(I had liv'd a blessed time)* if I had died before resolving to murder my King *(an hour before this chance),*" for the fall from the state of grace was coincident with the moral decision. "This chance," then, is the murder of Duncan, a notable fall. In the passage from *Hamlet* it is the tragic catastrophe. And the immediate emotional effect of this on the audience is said to be fear.

But fear is not the only effect ascribed to the catastrophe. In another passage the effects are designated as those of sorrow and astonishment, or woe and wonder. After the death of Hamlet, the young Fortinbras enters in the majesty of state, and as he enters asks:

> Where is this sight?

Horatio answers him:

> What is it you would see?
> If aught of woe or wonder, cease your search.
>
> 5. 2. 373-4

The tableau of destruction remains on the stage—

> O proud Death,
> What feast is toward in thine eternal cell
> That thou so many princes at a shot
> So bloodily hast struck?
>
> 5. 2. 375-8

And Horatio, who was privy to it all, defines this sight as one of woe and wonder, *doloris et admirationis.* It is interesting to note that in the First Quarto, the mangled stage version of *Hamlet,* the passage reads:

> enter Fortinbrasse with his traine.
> FORT.   Where is this bloody sight?
> HOR.   If aught of woe or wonder you'ld behold
> Then looke upon this tragicke spectacle.

In both texts the spectacle is characterized by its proper effects. One of these is *woe* or sorrow, which is the ground of pity, as it was to the Watch who discovered the bodies of Romeo and Juliet:

> We see the ground on which these woes do lie,
> But the true ground of all these piteous woes
> We cannot without circumstance descry.
>
> 5. 3. 179-81

19

Hence pity is evoked by the woes of the catastrophe of *Romeo*, the tragic deaths, by what the chorus-character, Friar Laurence, had already called in the same scene "this lamentable chance" (146). Nevertheless, woe is not precisely pity. It is the more general term, of which pity is a species. It is the English equivalent of that *dolor sive tristitia* which in the medieval tradition of literary criticism is noted, rather than pity *(misericordia sive commiseratio)*, as the subject and effect of tragedy,[7] and which in the medieval tradition of psychological analysis, which is substantially the Renaissance tradition, is treated at length along with fear as one of the basic and most powerful passions of the soul. The others are joy and hope (Thomas, *ST*, 1-2. 25.4).[8] Pity, then, denotes precisely the relationship of the spectator to the catastrophe; but the nature of the catastrophe itself is woeful.

The relationship of the terms is that expounded by Edgar in *Lear*. To Gloucester's question:

> Now, good sir, what are you?

he answers:

> A most poor man, made tame to fortune's blows,
> Who, by the art of known and feeling sorrows,
> Am pregnant to good pity.
>
> 4. 6. 224-7

If we may apply this passage to the general notion of tragedy, we may say that Edgar is the ideal spectator. He has attained the moral effect of that excitation of feeling; he has been "made tame" by participating in "fortune's blows," which are the material of tragedy; he has penetrated into that experience consciously and has realized its significance in feeling, and so has attained to the habit of, the capacity for exercising, the virtue of pity.

The catastrophe is sorrowful and naturally begets pity. It is also sudden, surprising, on a large scale, and involves great persons; hence it evokes wonder. This is an emotion less discussed in connection with tragedy than either fear or sorrow, and one that the literary person today does not easily think of as an emotion, but it is a commonplace in the Renaissance especially in connection with the deaths of notable persons and with the effects of drama and fiction. Dekker, for instance, with reference to the death of Queen Elizabeth, speaks of "the sorrow and amazement that like an earthquake began to shake the distempered body of this island (by reason of our late sovereign's departure)." And Sidney characterizes tragedy as "stirring the affects of admiration and commiseration."[9] *Admiration*, of course, is simply the Latin term for "wonder," as *commiseration* is for "pity." The emotion itself is that state of overpowering surprise, the shocked limit of feeling, which represents either the extreme of joy or, as in this case, the extreme of fear. Indeed, in the medieval tradition of psychological analysis it is defined as a species of fear (*ST*, 1-2. 41. 4), and thus the relation of wonder to fear is similar to that of pity to sorrow.

II

Fear, sorrow, and wonder are the explicit effects of the tragic catastrophe of *Hamlet,* or so at least it is here argued. But even if one grants that the effects are named in the particular passages cited, they are not spoken by the author in his own person. They are spoken by characters in a play. The remarks are in character, no doubt, and have some bearing on the delineation of character, but they can hardly be taken as expressing the author's intention with regard to the play as a whole, for drama by its very nature denies the author not only the right but even the possibility of speaking in his own person. Whatever a character thinks, says, or does must be taken only as an expression of character, and as an action in the sense that character and action are but aspects of each other. Hence Hamlet's remarks and Horatio's are elements in the

21

total effect of the play, functionally related to all other elements, but not to be taken as explicit comments which furnish a guiding principle of order for the whole and consequently represent the author's intention.

But the assumptions that lie behind this point of view do not apply to Elizabethan drama though they do apply to a good many modern works. The principal assumption is that the work as a whole is an indissoluble unit that exists only in its total effect. This is one aspect of the doctrine of organic form. The assumption operates in this way among others: whatever is said in a play is construed in the light of the critic's total impression of the work, or more often of the character who speaks since the delineation of character is usually taken to be the primary end of fiction. Hence a speech is first read as contributing to the whole, either of the play or of the character, and then reinterpreted so as to conform to the whole which the critic has constructed. Whatever is discordant with this must be reconciled, often by the invocation of "irony," a device as fertile as Stoic allegory for disposing of the difficulties which the original text puts in the way of an interpretation.

Now, if every speech of an effective character is dramatic, in the modern sense, then it never means what it says but is only an expression of what the critic thinks the character's character is. What this leads to in practice can be made clear by an example. A modern critic, and a scholar quite learned in Renaissance thought, sees in Iago's rejoinder to Roderigo's confession of moral helplessness (*Othello*, 1. 3. 319ff.) "a grand perversion of the theory that good is the end and purpose of reason."[10] Roderigo has confessed with a shameless determinism his love for Desdemona, even though she is Othello's wife:

> What should I do? I confess it is my shame to be so fond, but
> it is not in my virtue to amend it.

And Iago replies:

Virtue, a fig! 'Tis in ourselves that we are thus or thus. Our bodies are our gardens, to the which our wills are gardeners; so that if we will plant nettles or sow lettuce, set hyssop and weed up thyme, supply it with one gender of herbs or distract it with many—either to have it sterile with idleness or manured with industry—why, the power and corrigible authority of this lies in our wills.

The critic notes, "This passage states the ethics, the infidelity, of selfishness."

Perhaps he is misled by *Virtue, a fig!* (the punctuation is mine), overlooking the fact that in the context *(it is not in my virtue to amend it) virtue* has quite obviously the common Elizabethan meaning of "power," and that Iago is consequently by no means making light of that virtue which is the opposite of vice. For what does Iago say? He picks up Roderigo's assertion that it is not in his power not to be a sinning fool, to go kill himself for love, and maintains that we do have the power to make ourselves one thing or the other, good or evil, to control or not to control our bodies, our lower natures, and that this power is our will. This, so far as I can see, is a notorious commonplace of the Christian tradition, as well as of the Aristototelian. It is plain and hoary orthodoxy, and there is no perversion in it. Of course, a theologian might object that Iago's position is too Pelagian, that it makes no provision for the Grace of God, but the statement is brief and is not theological in context: in fact, you will hardly restrain a man from killing himself for love by suggesting that the Grace of God may prevent his accomplishing his purpose.

The second objection that could be made against the orthodoxy of this passage is that it is, perhaps, too voluntaristic, that nothing is said of reason. But this objection fails if we quote the whole passage, for Iago continues:

If the balance of our lives had not one scale of reason to poise another of sensuality, the blood and baseness of our natures would conduct us to most prepost'rous conclusions. But we

23

have reason to cool our raging motions, our carnal stings, our unbitted lusts; whereof I take this that you call love to be a sect or scion.

That is, Iago identifies the power and corrigible authority which lies in our wills with reason. Hence, it is evident that it is the medieval and Christian concept of the reasonable will which he opposes to the deterministic sensuality of Roderigo. Finally, no one, I trust, will maintain that Iago slanders in this instance true Love by designating Roderigo's infection as lust, which it is.

Yet on this latter passage the critic remarks: "Iago understands the warfare between reason and sensuality, but his ethics are totally inverted; reason works in him not good, as it should according to natural law, but evil, which he has chosen for his good." This, as a remark on Iago's character and actions in general, is aptly and accurately put. But the remark purports to be on this particular passage, and as such it is precisely wrong.

The passage is one of the finest statements, especially in its rhythm, of the traditional and orthodox view of the relation of the reasonable will to the sensitive soul; it has, then, its own absolute value as "thought," as the accomplished saying of something very much worth saying. It has also its function in the plot and its relation to Iago's character, but this function and relationship is rather "mechanical" (in fact, hierarchical) than "organic" (that is, monistic). Yet the passage serves the larger purposes of the plot without losing and altering its own quality as such. In the plot, it is an argument to persuade Roderigo from suicide, and is such an argument as a divine might use. But Iago's purpose in persuasion is not to save Roderigo's soul but to save his person and his purse for the benefit of Iago's own designs. The evil lies in the end, the intention; the means and the accidental effects are in themselves good, nor do they lose that quality in being used for an evil end. It is good to prevent a man from killing himself. The argument employed

24

is orthodox and true, and no less true for the circumstances. The devil quotes Scripture to his purpose, but you need not for this reason take Scripture as an expression of the devil's character.

A Shakespearean speech, then, takes its point in part from itself, especially if it goes beyond the bare gist of what is needed for the plot, and in part from its context, from who says it and under what circumstances. But the relation of context and speech is one that depends on relevant considerations, and relevance is construed in terms of what is appropriate. It is beside the point, then, in considering the last scene of *Hamlet*, that Hamlet occupies a privileged position among Shakespeare's heroes, that he is said to be of all those the most lovingly and sympathetically presented, so much so that many feel in this instance the author has been partial to his character. It is beside the point, even, that earlier in the play Hamlet has shown a critical interest in the discussion of drama. His remarks to the players are called forth by that situation and are appropriate to it, though they are also interesting in themselves and go quite beyond what is needed for the action.

It is somewhat in point that Hamlet is the hero, and especially that he is at the moment he speaks the sole surviving member of the royal family, and hence for that moment the head of the state; he has the right to speak authoritatively. Besides, he is dying, and one's last words are commonly supposed to be truthful. But the real point is that his remarks are addressed to the standers-by as to an audience. They are a comment on the reactions of an audience, and must be taken as expressing how an audience would and should react. His remarks simply put into words what the other actors on the stage are to express in gesture, and if the actual audience does not feel the like, the play has been a failure.

The character of Horatio, however, and the circumstances under which he speaks are, in this respect, a little more complicated. In the first place, he speaks at the request of Fortinbras. And what is the significance of Fortinbras? He is the principle of renewed order in the state. He is the indispensable character for concluding a Shakespearean play; for each play, with the notable exception of *Troilus and Cressida,* begins with disorder in the state and concludes only on the restoration of order. As the representative of order he is in virtue of his office conceived of as reason: for authority is order, and order is reason. This is common doctrine. He speaks the truth and the truth is spoken to him. Consequently, his presence is almost a necessary condition for Horatio's remarks.

But what is the position of Horatio himself? Horatio, as has often been noted, is a kind of chorus. He is a special character outside of the plot, except in so far as he is the confidant of and spokesman for Hamlet. But he is not the kind of chorus that is swayed now to this side and now to that as the tides of sympathy and fortune shift, as is the Greek chorus, or the chorus in Jonson's *Cataline.* Horatio is the well-tempered man. He is the man of whom Hamlet has said:

> Since my dear soul was mistress of her choice
> And could of men distinguish, her election
> Hath seal'd thee for herself. For thou hast been
> As one, in suff'ring all, that suffers nothing;
> A man that Fortune's buffets and rewards
> Hath ta'en with equal thanks; and blest are those
> Whose blood and judgement are so well commingled
> That they are not a pipe for Fortune's finger
> To sound what stop she please. Give me that man
> That is not passion's slave, and I will wear him
> In my heart's core, ay, in my heart of hearts,
> As I do thee.
>
> 3. 2. 68-79

This speech has its own function in the scene—it is the play scene— and it serves particularly as a contrast with the later bitter ragging of Rosencrantz and Guildenstern: "You would play upon me; you would seem to know my stops; you would pluck out the heart of my mystery . . . ," and so on (3. 2. 380ff.). It has its own function as a thought worthy of being expressed and not inappropriate to the circumstances. But it is also the speech that establishes in fairly full and explicit terms the relevance of Horatio to the play.

One of the key terms in the passage is *election*. This is a technical term in the medieval tradition for the act of moral choice (*ST*, 1-2, 13, translating Aristotle's *proairesis*) with respect to choosing the means to an end. The end is happiness, or some aspect of it, and true friendship with a just man is the means—

> Horatio, thou art e'en as just a man
> As e'er my conversation cop'd withal.
>
> 3. 2. 59-60

Thus election chooses Horatio. But moral choice is a function of reason, of the soul, and is exercised as soon as one attains the "age of reason," but not before (*ST*, 1. 100. 2, and 1-2. 13. 2. *contra*). Finally, the metaphor of sealing derives from the common Aristotelian and scholastic figure of imposing a seal on wax, which represents the relationship of form and matter: the choice of means gives determinate form to the end desired (*ST*, 1-2. 13. 1. c., especially *ad fin.*). The meaning is illustrated in the following passage:

> NESTOR.   . . . It is suppos'd
> He that meets Hector issues from our choice;
> And choice, being mutual act of all our souls,
> Makes merit her election . . .
>
> *Troilus*, 1. 3. 346-9

Choice is an act of the soul; the particular act of choosing this or this as means is *election*. Sometimes the choice is erroneous, the will is carried away by the sensitive appetite (*ST*, 1-2 .77):

> HECTOR. But value dwells not in particular will:
> It holds his estimate and dignity
> As well wherein 'tis precious of itself
> As in the prizer. 'Tis mad idolatry
> To make the service greater than the god;
> And the will dotes that is attributive
> To what infectiously itself affects
> Without some image of th'affected merit.
> TROILUS. I take to-day a wife, and my election
> Is led on in the conduct of my will,
> My will enkindled by mine eyes and ears,
> Two traded pilots 'twixt the dangerous shores,
> Of will and judgement. How may I avoid,
> Although my will distaste what it elected,
> The wife I chose? . . .
>
> *Troilus*, 2. 2. 53-67

Similarly in *Cymbeline*:

> SECOND LORD. If it be a sin to make a true election
> She is damn'd.
>
> 1. 2. 29-30

To return, Hamlet says that Horatio is the man whom Hamlet, when he comes to the age of reason, selected by a reasonable choice as the fit co-respondent of his dear soul, which is in its essence reason. For Horatio is one who is open to all experience but who suffers by it no inner alteration of his reasonable form. He is impassive to all passions. He is indifferent to the external operations of fortune, for he is a man of perfected self-mastery, sealed by grace, in whom the irrational and the rational are in due relation, the one subordinated to the other; and thus the inner unalterable core of reasonable order is not subject to the irrational alterations produced by the impingement of external circumstances. Hence Horatio should be regarded as the ideal commentator, like the similar characters in Jonson's plays, Cordatus, Crites, and Horace: he is reason expressing reasonable judgment on the action.

28

The point perhaps calls for some elaboration. The ideal spokesman in Elizabethan literature is always spokesman by virtue of his reasonableness. He is never intended to be biographically identifiable with the author, though of course it would be impossible for authors so individual as Shakespeare and Jonson not to infuse some of their own qualities into a character. But the Elizabethan author had no intention of expressing his own personality, either in a character or in his work as a whole. In fact, he did not know that he had such a thing as a personality, for the concept of personality can hardly be said to have been formed. It was the reasonable soul that was the central psychological concept of the Renaissance, and a man was praiseworthy, as Horatio was, in so far as the reasonable soul spoke in him and was hearkened to. It is true that a man was considered to have certain individualising properties derived from his sex, his time of life, and his position in society, but these were comprised in the concept of decorum. They were the differentiations of reasonableness in accordance with circumstance. Whatever traits he might have beyond these, as for instance, melancholy or foppery, were the result of a disturbance of reasonable balance and a deviation from the ideal norm, and they were vicious in so far as they deviated. All this is familiar to the student of the Renaissance, but the conclusion is that the character who is presented as conforming to the ideal norm is presented as a standard by which deviations from the norm may be charted, and when he speaks he speaks in the light of reason, and what he says represents the author's explicit intentions. For the author himself is reason.

IV

The question of under what circumstances Horatio speaks has now been answered in part. He speaks in reply to Fortinbras' request, and Fortinbras is the principle of reason and order in the state, who expounds and exacts the truth; and he himself is the reasonable commentator.

But the situation is more complicated than this. The situation at the end of *Hamlet* is the kind of final one which is customary in Shakespeare's plays. The loose ends, or most of them, are now tied up; the course of action is recapitulated and in part explained; and the representative of the state invites the principal remaining characters to "go hence, to have more talk of these sad things" (*Romeo,* 5. 3. 307), "where we may leisurely / Each one demand and answer to his part" (*Winter's Tale.* 5. 3. 152-3). But in *Hamlet* this basic situation is given a curious expansion and development.

We have already seen how Hamlet treats the cast on the stage as spectators of the catastrophe, and have quoted the passage in which he turns to Horatio, and, as it were, deputizes him. He lays on Horatio the charge "to tell my story," a charge which Horatio accepts when he proposes later to "speak to th' yet unknowing world / How these things came about." Indeed Fortinbras accepts the proposal: "Let us haste to hear it," he says, "And call the noblest to the audience" (5. 2. 360, 390, 397-8).

The lines are so familiar that the reader may not notice what is happening. It is implied in a series of ambiguities, as was implied more openly in Hamlet's speech, that the minor characters who remain on the stage are to be regarded as an audience. Such a notion is involved in Fortinbras' pun, to "call the noblest to the audience," for they shall attend the audience of the new king, and they shall be an audience to whom the events will be related. In like fashion, Horatio asks, before he begins his resumé of the plot, that orders be given that the bodies of the main characters in the catastrophe "High on a stage be placed to the view"; these bodies, then, which are to be placed on a ceremonial stage become by virtue of an obvious pun the characters who will act on a theatrical stage. For the difference between Hamlet's relation to his quasi-audience and Horatio's is this: the other characters are treated by Hamlet as spectators of the events which just took place on the stage; they are treated by Horatio as spectators or auditors of the events that he is about to recount or present. Horatio, who has been deputized by Hamlet to tell his story, is treated in the end almost as if he were the author of the play of *Hamlet*. The events which we have just seen on the stage are treated according to the usual dramatic convention as if they had just now really happened. They are reality, and the play about this reality will only begin when the play we have seen is over.

Thus Horatio, who is about to give an account of these events, is the imitator and expounder of the reality we have seen. It is in keeping with this curious sleight-of-hand that, in preparation for the play which will follow the final bare stage, Horatio presents the argument of the events in a kind of prologue:

> . . . give order that these bodies
> High on a stage be placed to the view;
> And let me speak to th' yet unknowing world
> How these things came about. So shall you hear
> Of carnal, bloody, and unnatural acts;
> Of accidental judgements, casual slaughters;
> Of deaths put on by cunning and forc'd cause,
> And, in this upshot, purposes mistook
> Fall'n on th' inventors' heads. All this can I
> Truly deliver.
>
> 5. 2. 388-97

The passage is in effect a summary of the preceding action. It is in form an argument of the relation which is supposed to follow, and it has the stylistic qualities of the conventional argument. But what is more—it is the truth: "All this can I truly deliver," for I am the repository of Hamlet's trust, I am the reasonable man and hence the ideal spokesman, I am the intention of the author.

Consequently, Horatio's *Hamlet* is also Shakespeare's *Hamlet*. Each is constituted by the plot, by what happens. Each

31

is concerned with "carnal, bloody, and unnatural acts," and these are, respectively, the adultery, murder, and incest which precede and lay the foundation for the play. The accidental judgment which leads to the casual slaughter is Hamlet's mistaking Polonius for the King, a judgment based upon misconstrued signs and hence not a true or substantial judgment. This is clear to anyone who is familiar with the scholastic discussion of manslaughter, or casual homicide. To employ the Latin terminology which Shakespeare uses in its anglicized form, this judgment *per accidens* leads to a slaughter which is *praeter intentionem,* and so casual, not causal *(ST,* 2-2. 64. 8).

Perhaps the idea here deserves a short digression. It appears again in an extraordinary passage in the *Winter's Tale.* Florizel says, in reply to the question, "Have you thought on a place whereto you'll go?" after marrying Perdita:

> Not any yet;
> But as th'unthought-on accident is guilty
> To what we wildly do, so we profess
> Ourselves to be the slaves of chance and flies
> Of every wind that blows.

> 4. 4. 548-52

The philosophy, no doubt, is too great for the occasion, but there is no reason to assume that it is not pertinent. Nevertheless, this is surely an odd passage, and the oddness lies in the comparison, in the *as* clause. For, to profess oneself the slave of chance and fly of every wind that blows is a common notion and fairly easy to understand: it is an indulgence often granted to young lovers by those whom their actions are not liable to hurt. But the notion is qualified by the preceding clause: we are the slaves of chance, Florizel says, in the sense in which the unthought-on accident is guilty to what we wildly do. What does this mean?

It depends on the distinction in casuistry which is drawn in Horatio's phrase above, that between causal and casual actions.

32

The distinction is especially clear in the discussions of actions which arise from drunkenness, or any similar state of "wildly doing." For example, if a man gets drunk and in that state "unintentionally" kills another, he is not directly guilty of homicide spiritually, whatever he may be legally, for the result is beyond his intention. But he does not on this account get off spiritually easily. He is guilty of such a degree of irrational drunkenness as rendered the homicide possible, or even probable. The substance of his sin, then, lay in the choice by which he came into the condition of "wildly doing." The example is St. Thomas'. Hooker in the *Laws of Ecclesiastical Polity* deals with an analogous case:

> Finally, that which we do being evil, is notwithstanding by so much more pardonable, by how much the exigence of so doing or the difficulty of doing otherwise is greater; unless this necessity or difficulty have originally arisen from ourselves. It is no excuse therefore unto him, who being drunk committeth incest, and allegeth that his wits were not his own; inasmuch as himself might have chosen whether his wits should by that mean have been taken from him.   1. 9. 1[11]

In brief, then, the initial choice is intentional; the precise consequences may be accidental and the result of chance. Such is the scheme of thought that lies behind the *as* clause. The initial choice of going off with Perdita is within Florizel's power, and he will make it, for he has embraced the condition of "wildly doing":

> FLORIZEL. From my succession wipe me, father! I
>   Am heir to my affection.
> CAMILLO. Be advis'd.
> FLORIZEL. I am, and by my fancy. If my reason
>   Will thereto be obedient, I have reason;
>   If not, my sense, better pleas'd with madness,
>   Do bid it welcome.
> CAMILLO. This is desperate, sir.
>
>   4. 4. 491-6

He is heir to his emotions; he is advised by imagination to which his reason must subscribe. Hence what follows, as particularly the place whereto they'll go, will be accidental and the result of chance. It will be, like the death of Polonius, casual.

But to return to Horatio's speech in *Hamlet*—the "deaths put on by cunning and forced cause" are, of course, the deaths of Rosencrantz and Guildenstern, and "this upshot" in which the intrigue with dramatic justice recoils on the intriguers is the final scene of the play.

There is obviously a point for point correspondence between the items of Horatio's list and the main events of the central plot of *Hamlet*. However, the items themselves are not particularized as in the traditional argument, but generalized.[12] No names are mentioned, no particular circumstances alluded to. And the generalization is pointed by the consistent use of the generalized plural: *acts, judgements, slaughters, deaths, purposes, inventors*; for, though some of these items may be considered to be proper plurals, it is significant that all are pluralized. The items listed are such classes of action as generally form the subject-matter of tragedy. They do not precisely correspond to, but they are of the same nature as, the items in the Donatan tradition, or in, for example, Scaliger's list of the subject-matters of tragedy: "The matters of tragedy are great and terrible, as commands of kings, slaughters, despairs, suicides, exiles, bereavements, parricides, incests, conflagrations, battles, the putting out of eyes, weeping, wailing, bewailing, funerals, eulogies, and dirges." Nor are such lists simply to be found in critical treatises: they are the common property of the times. Mr. Harding in his theological controversy with Bishop Jewel seizes the occasion of Jewel's mention of Sophocles to insert a summary description of tragedy. "A tragedy," he says, "setteth forth the overthrows of kingdoms, murder of noble personages, and other great troubles, and endeth in woful lamentations." And Jewel retorts with a full list of the

34

terrible tragic events associated with the villainous Popes of Rome.[13]

In brief, Horatio promises his audience a tragedy. "So shall you hear," he says—and then follows a generalized list of items which every member of the audience recognized at once as equivalent to the single word—"tragedy." The implication is that *Hamlet* is a tragedy because it presents such tragic actions. Furthermore, the effects of tragedy which Shakespeare mentions in this scene—pity, fear, astonishment—arise from the nature of the tragic actions themselves, for these actions are, as Scaliger says, great and terrible, and they evoke a corresponding response. They are terrible in that they are great, and pitiable and wonderful for the same reason. Such an equation between the greatness of the persons and the action and the greatness of the tragic response is explicitly formulated in the final comment of Octavius, the representative of the state at the conclusion of *Antony and Cleopatra:*

> High events as these
> Strike those that make them; and their story is
> No less in pity than his glory which
> Brought them to be lamented.
>
> 5. 2. 363-6.

A tragedy, then, is defined by the kind of actions it presents, and the effect of tragedy is the direct result of the presentation of such actions, though the validity of the effect may depend upon other considerations. The effect, moreover, is one of fear, sorrow, and wonder. This is no doubt a relatively crude aesthetic, but it is substantially Aristotle's, and it is Shakespeare's. It is also true.

III

The Donatan Tradition

Fear, sorrow, and wonder are the emotions explicitly associated with tragedy, not only in *Hamlet*, but generally in the tradition of literary criticism of Shakespeare's day. The tradition is well-known. It derives from a few time-worn texts which were repeated with the singlemindedness with which one recites the penny catechism.[1]

I

The basic text for the theory of tragedy comes from a schoolbook of the late classical period, Donatus on Terence:

> There are many differences between tragedy and comedy, but the principal difference is that in comedies the characters are of moderate estate, the difficulties that arise are slight, and the outcome of it all is joyful; but the marks of tragedy are precisely the opposite; the characters are great, the actions fearful in the extreme, and the outcome is sad and involves deaths. Again, in comedy all is disturbed at the beginning and tranquil at the close; in tragedy the order of progression is exactly reversed. The moral of tragedy is that life should be rejected; of comedy, that it should be embraced. And, finally, in comedy the story is always made-up; in tragedy, the story is commonly true and based on history.[2]

Tragedy and comedy are precise contraries; from this center the particular marks of distinction are evolved and disposed. Such a way of looking at things was quite congenial to the medieval mind, whose basic discipline was the logic of Aristotle and the principles of identity, contradiction, and the law of the excluded middle, and whose view of men was conditioned by the doctrine of Heaven and Hell, good and evil, grace and sin, and of the irreparable differences between them. There went along with this the clarity of definition and discrimination which this habit of mind encouraged. If the clarity broke down in practice, if in the hurly-burly of the stage comedy intruded on tragedy, this could only be ascribed, so long as the habit of mind persisted, to the imperfect nature of man which it was the duty of thought and intention to remedy. Hence tragicomedy, for example, did not pose a practical problem since it was actually in existence, nor a problem of authority since it had the warrant of Plautus, but a logical problem, and almost an insuperable one, for the two elements were defined by their opposition.

The distinctions which Donatus establishes between the two forms are firmly held throughout the tradition. They are distinctions of 1) character, 2) order of progression in the plot, 3) source and kind of plot, 4) moral purpose, 5) kind of incident and the accompanying emotional effect, 6) kind of conclusion and the accompanying emotional effect, together with three additional principles stated in other texts than Donatus — 7) the nature of the subject matter, 8) the principle which accounts for the turn in the fortune of the characters, and 9) the nature of the style. Several of these imply each other, and a few corollary distinctions enter in the later tradition, but on the whole these principles, the first six of which are clearly stated in Donatus, sufficiently characterize the tradition and amply account for the nature of tragedy on the Elizabethan stage. Indeed, if these distinctions are taken seriously and regarded as principles of order by which the dramatist writes as he does rather than as rules external to the work, it will be seen that Elizabethan tragedy, including Hamlet, is in large part given merely by the acceptance of these principles. It follows that the historian of Elizabethan drama might more plausibly begin with the traditional definition than with the earliest examples of medieval drama. The latter are historical forerunners which only in small part account for the developed product; the definition is almost the Archetype itself, in which the seminal ideas, the principles of order, explicitly dwell.

The first distinction is that the tragic characters must be great, and this means of high rank. It is the modern feeling that this is an artificial stipulation, explicable only in light of the erroneous social ideas of our ancestors. But *The Death of a Salesman* is not a tragedy in the old sense, and so one might conjecture there is something else involved: there is involved a radical difference in the nature of the tragic effect. For the field of tragedy will be the state, since men of high rank are rulers of the state. Tragedy will then involve not private life and private feeling—this is the province of comedy —, but public life and public feeling. But public feeling is different in kind from private.[3] A public calamity moves us in a different way than does a private one. The murder of John Doe is one thing; the assassination of Trotsky or of Admiral Darlan is another. Hence the tragic emotions in the older tradition will be predominantly communal and public, and we will find that a similar qualification is implied in the other principles of order which Donatus distinguishes.

The second distinction is that the direction of the action in tragedy is from order to disorder; in comedy the converse. How deeply this scheme had entered into Shakespeare's thought can be conjectured from the passage in *Lear* in which it forms the structural framework of the expression. Edgar soliloquizes on the heath:

> To be worst,
> The lowest and most dejected thing of fortune,
> Stands still in esperance, lives not in fear.
> The lamentable change is from the best;
> The worst returns to laughter.
>
> 4. 1. 2-6

The change appropriate to tragedy *(the lamentable change)* is from the best; the change from the worst is comedy. Yet Shakespearean tragedy does not exhibit this progression in its

38

simple form. The greater part of a Shakespearean tragedy does, it is true, consist of a progression toward deeper and deeper disorder, but a) the beginning is not tranquil since there is already some disorder (as in the opening scenes of *Romeo*, *Hamlet*, and *Othello*), and b) the end always involves (with the curious exception of *Troilus* whose literary form is still a matter of dispute) the restoration of order and tranquility. That is, the principle is clearly operative, but under certain limitations.

We can see, however, why the limitations are introduced. a) Since the play deals with disorder, it is simple craftsmanship to begin with at least the first motions of disorder, and if a traditional precept be needed, Horace is at hand with the admonition to begin in the middle of things, which Shakespeare himself invokes in the prologue to *Troilus*. b) As for the conclusion, the concept of order was of such importance to Shakespeare and his contemporaries, and politically of such importance, that we may assume that he neither cared to end a play in disorder (except for *Troilus*), nor perhaps would he have felt safe in so doing. But beyond this, order at the end of such harrowing experiences as constitute tragedy implies an intention to communicate to the spectators a commensurate order in feeling—by a tranquil close to dismiss them in calm of mind, all passion spent. But this calm of mind is correlative with order in the state: the aesthetic feeling is in part political in nature.[4]

The third distinction is that the plot of tragedy is commonly historical and true, not feigned. We can understand, then, the fusion of the historical chronicle play and tragedy in Elizabethan drama, for it has its critical justification in this tenet. But if tragedy is historical, it is not merely realistic as distinguished from being fanciful; it has rather the compelling absoluteness of accomplished fact. Hence its effect will be accompanied by the recognition that things could not be otherwise, since this is how in fact they were. It follows from this, as from the principles of high rank in personages and of concluding order in the state, that the emotional effects of tragedy will be of a kind consonant with these requirements. They will be more impersonal than personal. The experiences which the spectator will associate with these effects, the traces and memories which will give them substance, will be drawn not from the guarded and private world of his sensibility, but from the more communal world of his public self. The content of the effects will thus be different in kind from that which the uninstructed modern reader will experience, and a comparable difference in kind is implied in the next principle.

This, the fourth, is the moral purpose of tragedy. Donatus tells us that the lesson expressed in tragedy is the rejection of life *(fugienda vita)*. Thus, in a Christian and political context tragedy will be regarded as a warning against pride and against trusting in worldly prosperity. Sidney, for example, maintains that tragedy "with stirring the affects of admiration and commiseration teacheth the uncertainty of this world and upon how weak foundations gilden roofs are builded";[5] and Jonson closes *Sejanus* with these massive reflections:

> Let this example move th' insolent man
> Not to grow proud and careless of the gods.
> It is an odious wisdom to blaspheme,
> Much more to slighten or deny their powers;
> For whom the morning saw so great and high,
> Thus low and little fore the even doth lie.

But if one takes into account the subsequent principles in Donatus' definition, the fifth, that the incidents of tragedy involve great fears, and the sixth, that the catastrophe involves deaths and is sorrowful *(exitus funesti)*, it will be clear that resignation to death in the Christian sense is the natural moral to such tragedy. It is, in fact, the moral of *Hamlet*, expressed by the hero as he goes to the catastrophe, disturbed by forebodings of the tragic issue:

we defy augury; there's a special providence in the fall of a sparrow. If it be now, 'tis not to come; if it be not to come, it will be now; if it be not now, yet it will come: the readiness is all.

5. 2. 230-3

Such acquiescence, if we should take the Donatan moral seriously, would constitute the catharsis of this kind of tragedy, the effect of the tragic effect. It would be one of logic and theology, whose instrument is teaching, and whose end is Christian resignation.

But what must be the nature of the emotional effects themselves if they are to conduce to such an end? They must be impersonal to a marked degree. For resignation is the subsumption, and almost the loss, of the individual under the general. One's own death cannot be a matter of frightened concern, since it is not peculiar but common, since it is inevitable and given. So Caesar:

> Of all the wonders that I yet have heard,
> It seems to me most strange that men should fear,
> Seeing that death, a necessary end,
> Will come when it will come.

Julius Caesar, 2. 2. 34-7

And Gertrude to Hamlet:

> Thou know'st 'tis common. All that lives must die,
> Passing through nature to eternity.

1. 2. 72-3

Thus the emotional disturbance of tragic incident is resolved in resignation.

The process is traditional in Christianity. Thomas Aquinas, for example (*ST*, 1-2. 42. 2. ad 3) tells us that death and other lapses of Nature have Universal Nature, or Eternal Law, as cause; but the nature of a particular being fights against such lapses as much as it can, and from this striving springs sorrow and anguish when death is seen as present, fear and

41

terror when it looms in the future. These are the tragic emotions, and aroused by the tragic fact of death. Resignation in this tradition is nothing other than the acquiescence of Particular in Universal Nature. It is nothing other than an effective belief in logic, so that to perceive the subsumption of instance under rule is to be satisfied. If all men are mortal, then Hamlet, being a man, is also mortal.

But emotional effects that are ordered toward acquiescence, disturbances that are intended to subside, are different in kind from those that are exploitable and are intended to be enjoyed. The latter are sentimental and private; the former are in potency to the impersonal order of their envisaged end.

II

A tragedy is a succession of fearful incidents, enacted by persons of high rank, that progresses from initial calm into ever-deepening disaster, and concludes sadly in deaths. Fear and sorrow are its appropriate emotions, fear of the catastrophe and sorrow at its accomplishment. They are appropriate because they are the natural emotions with which men regard death in prospect and in fulfilment. They are, furthermore, emotions of a public and impersonal order.

The similarity of this definition to that of Aristotle's *Poetics* is obvious, and in all likelihood the tradition derives partly from Aristotle himself, if not from the *Poetics* (which seems to have been little known in Antiquity and to have been recovered in the West only in the Thirteenth Century), then from his lost dialogue *On Poets* and from his student Theophrastus and the Peripatetic School. From such sources the tradition descended to the Alexandrian and Roman scholars, and from them to the school texts of late Antiquity.[6] But the history is not important in this connection. What is important is that these notions entered into the texture of medieval thought, and came to the Renaissance as commonplaces. Hence,

I shall present now a few additional texts in which may be distinguished certain further and corollary principles of order, together with a text from the late Middle Ages and one from Shakespeare's day in which can be seen the consistency of the tradition and the liveliness of reapprehension with which it was entertained two thousand years after Aristotle.

Of equal importance with that of Donatus is the definition of Diomedes, a grammarian of the Fourth Century A.D.:

> Tragedy involves the full cycle of fortune turning to adversity in characters of the heroic age—this is Theophrastus' definition. . . . Comedy—we render the Greek definition—involves a full cycle in the fortune of private citizens, but never the danger of death. . . . The fortunes involved in comedy are those of little streets and unimportant households, not as in tragedy of princes and men of state. . . . The distinctions between comedy and tragedy are these: the characters of tragedy are semi-divine, leaders of the state, kings; those of comedy are unimportant and private persons. The subjects of tragedy are woes, exiles, deaths; of comedy, love affairs and seductions. Finally, the movement of events in tragedy is almost always from happy circumstances to bitter deaths, accompanied at the end with the perception that the fortunes of the house involved have gone to ruin. Hence comedy and tragedy are by definition distinct: the one a full cycle of harmless incident, the other a reversal of great fortunes. Sorrow, then, is characteristic of tragedy.
>
> *Ars Grammatica,* 3[7]

To this may be added two passages from Isidore of Seville's encyclopedia, the *Britannica* of ten centuries. The first is from the section "On Poets":

> The tragic writers have attained considerable fame, principally for the plots of their plays, which are fashioned in the image of truth. . . . The comic writers deal with the lives of private citizens; the tragic, however, with affairs of state and the histories

of kings. Similarly, the plots of tragedies deal with woful material; of comedies, with happy.

Etymologiae, 8. 7. 5-6

The second passage is from the section "On Shows":

> Tragedians are those who recite to an audience a lamentable poem about historical events and the crimes of wicked princes.

18. 45

As early as the tenth century this is contracted into the curt phrase: *tragoedia luctuosum carmen*. Tragedy is a lamentable tale, a woful story. To these texts may be added the influential sentence from Boethius' *Consolation of Philosophy*: *quid tragoediarum clamor aliud deflet nisi indiscreto ictu fortunam felicia regna vertentem?* which Chaucer translates:

> What other thyng bywalen the cryinges of tragedyes but oonly the dedes of Fortune that with unwar strook overturneth the realmes of great nobleye? *(Glose. Tragedye is to seyn a dite of a prosperite for a tyme, that endeth in wrecchidness.)*

2. Prose 2

together with Ovid's remark, "Tragedy is weightier in style than any other genre" (*Tristia*, 2. 381).

From these texts we may distinguish some additional principles of order. The seventh defines the range of subject matter: woes, exiles, slaughter, the crimes and villainies of princes, the ruin of a noble house, the downfall of kingdoms. The eighth defines the organization of the plot, which describes a period, a full circle, so that the tragic character may say at the end as Edmund says in *Lear:*

> The wheel is come full circle; I am here.

5. 3. 174

The principle of alteration, the power that turns the circle of prosperity, is Fortune, whose indiscriminate blow overturns prosperous kingdoms. The importance of this principle is well-known and generally conceded. It accounts for the dominant conception of tragedy in the late Middle Ages and the Renaissance, that tragedy is the fall from prosperity of a character of high estate.

A classic example is Marlowe's *Edward II*, where in the final scene the Queen says to Mortimer:

> Now, Mortimer, begins our tragedy.
>
> 2591

And the nature of the tragedy is defined a few lines later by Mortimer himself:

> Base Fortune, now I see that in thy wheel
> There is a point to which when men aspire
> They tumble headlong down. That point I touched,
> And, seeing there was no place to mount up higher,
> Why should I grieve at my declining fall?
> Farewell, fair Queen, weep not for Mortimer
> That scorns the world and, as a traveller,
> Goes to discover countries yet unknown.
>
> 2627-34

The fall in this case is followed by Mortimer's death, and in general the tragic fall is consummated by death, so that the principle of Fortune and the principle of death are identified. Nevertheless, it is probably significant to ascertain upon which of the two emphasis is laid: here the emphasis is clearly on the fall; in Shakespeare it is clearly on death. Furthermore, the fall is generally sudden and absolute: note Chaucer's mistranslation as "unwar strook," or unforeseen, of *indiscreto ictu*, which means "a random stroke." This introduces the element of surprise, which will in part account for the addition of the effect of wonder, and which will obviously serve to transfer the effect of fear from the incidents that precede the catastrophe to the catastrophe itself.

The ninth is the principle of style: tragedy requires the weighty or high style, a requirement which is implied by the principle of decorum—

> But to present a kingly troop withal,
> Give me a stately-written tragedy,
> *Tragoedia cothurnata,* fitting kings,
> Containing matter, and not common things.
> *Spanish Tragedy.* 4. 154-7

For, only the high style in its aspect of gravity is fitted to deal with affairs of state, and only the high style in its aspect of forceful utterance, of passion and vividness, is fitted to deal with crimes and villanies, and to call forth the terror, the woe, and especially the wonder which it is the peculiar function of high rhetoric to produce.

These texts, with others which need not be cited here, were copied again and again throughout the Middle Ages, repeatedly glossed, and indeed became so trite and common-place that they can scarcely be said to have a history, only a continued and recurrent existence. One example will suffice to illustrate the continuation. It is a passage from Lydgate's *Troy Book* (about 1420) in which he develops a remark by Guido delle Colonne to the effect that tragedies and comedies were said to have been first acted at Troy:

> And first also, I rede, that in Troye
> Wer song and rad lusty fresche comedies,
> And other dites, that called be tragedies.
> And to declare, schortly in sentence   845
> Of bothe two the final difference:
> A comedie hath in his gynning,
> At prime face, a maner compleyning,
> And afterward endeth in gladnes;
> And it the dedis only doth express   850
> Of swiche as ben in pouert plounged lowe;
> But tragidie, who so list to knowe,
> It begynneth in prosperite,
> And endeth euer in aduersity;
> And it also doth the conquest trete   855
> Of riche kynges and of lordys grete,
> Of mighty men and olde conquerou[ri]s,

46

Whiche by fraude of Fortunys schowris
Ben ouercast and whelmed from her glorie
Of a Theatyre stondynge in the princypale
paleys of Troye, declarenge the falle of
Pryncys and others.
And whilon thus was halwed the memorie   860
Of tragedies, as bokis make minde,
Whan thei wer rad or songyn, as I fynde,
In the theatre ther was a smal auter
Amyddes set, that was half circuler,
Whiche in-to the Est of custom was directe;   865
Up-on the whiche a pulpet was erecte,
And ther-in stod an aw[n]cien poete,
For to reherese by rhetorikes swete
The noble dedis, that wer historial,
Of kynges, princes for a memorial,   870
And of thes olde, worthi Emperours,
The grete emprises eke of conquerours,
And how thei gat in Martis high honour
The laurer grene for fyn of her labour,
The palm of knyghthod disservid by [old] date,   875
Or Parchas mad hem passyn in-to fate.
And after that, with chere and face pale,
With stile enclyned gan to turne his tale,
And for to synge, after al her loos,
Ful mortally the stroke of Antropos,   880
And telle also, for al her worthihede,
The sodeyn brekyng of her lives threde:
How pitiously thei made her mortal ende
Thorugh fals Fortune, that al the world will schende,
And how the fyn of al her worthines   885
Endid in sorwe and in highe tristesse,
By compassyng of fraude or fals tresoun,
By sodeyn mordre or vengaunce of poysoun,
Or conspirynge of fretyng fals envye,
How unwarly that thei dide dye;   890
And how her renoun and her highe fame
Was of hatrede sodeynly made lame;

And how her honour drowe un-to decline;
And the meschef of her unhappy fyne;
And how Fortune was to hem unswete—   895
Al this was tolde and rad of the poete,
And whil that he in the pulpet stood,
With dedly face al devoide of blood,
Singinge his dites, with muses al to-rent,
Amydde the theatre schrowdid in a tent,   900
Ther cam out men gastful of her cheris,
Disfigurid her facis with viseris,
Pleying by signes in the peples sight,
That the poete songon hath on hight;
So that ther was no maner discordaunce   905
Atwen his dites and her contenaunce:
For lik as he aloft[e] dide expresse
Wordes of Ioye or of heuynes,
Meving and cher, bynethe of hem pleying,
From point to point was alwey answering—   910
Now trist, now glad, now hevy, and [now] light,
And face chaunged with a sodeyn sight,
So craftily thei koude hem transfigure,
Conformyng hem to the chaunt[e]plure,
Now to synge and sodeinly to wepe,   915
So wel thei koude her observaunces kepe . . . [8]

Here are all the elements of the tradition, though jumbled
together and in no particular order. The concept of tragedy is
essentially determined, as it is in Donatus and Diomedes, by
contrast with the concept of comedy (845-6). Tragedy begins
happily and ends in adversity (852 ff.); the external principle of
the reversal is Fortune (858-9; 884; 895); the characters are
rich kings and great lords (856); tragedy is rhetorical (868),
that is, in high style — "stile enclyned" (878) —, and in
verse (844); the subject-matter is historical (869); the narrator clearly displays fear (877) and this is associated with the
rhetorical manner and with the subject of death (878 ff.); in

fact, the terror w. ·h the narrator displays "with dedly face al devoide of blooɑ as he tears the cat ("the muses al to-rente") in bombastic high style is mirrored in the pantomime of the dumb-show, and, in general, there is an exact correspondence between the fear, sorrow, emotional excitation ("meving"), and the joy of the text and of the illustrative action, together with a considerable range in the emotions called forth (897-916). Furthermore, the catastrophe is piteous (883) and sorrowful (886); it is sudden (882), and is brought about by violence and deceit — fraud, false treason, sudden murder, the vengeance of poison, or the conspiracy of biting envy (887-9); in fact, the tragic catastrophe is precisely sudden and violent death (880 ff.).

But here are also most of the elements of Elizabethan tragedy, and some which, though corollaries to the principles enunciated in the earlier tradition, are not explicit there. For example: if Marlowe's *Tamburlaine* is a tragical discourse and its presentation a "tragic glass," as it is called on the title-page and in the prologue to the original edition, this is because the play is in high style and as Lydgate here says:

> doth the conquest trete
> Of riche kynges and of lordys grete,
> Of mighty men and olde conquerou[ri]s.

The introduction of the notion of the "conspiringe of fretyng fals envye" as engineering the tragic catastrophe will help account — to choose one example among many — for the curious circumstance that the debate between Comedy and Tragedy in the Induction to the popular Elizabethan play of *Mucedorus* is conducted by Comedy and by Envy, who speaks for tragedy. It accounts also for many an Elizabethan play, particularly for the motivation of *Othello* and of Jonson's *Sejanus*. The concern for the honor and reputation of the protagonist after his tragic death is peculiarly relevant to the last scene of *Hamlet*. The "vengaunce of poysoun" is *Hamlet* again. Finally, the confusion of high style with bombast — "the muses al to-rente" — is markedly Elizabethan; the first we hear of Shakespeare in London is that — as Greene querulously complains — he thinks he can bombast out a blank verse with the best of them, even as Hamlet later thinks he can swing it as well as Laertes — "Nay, an thou'lt mouth, / I'll rant as well as thou" (5. 1. 306-7). In brief, if the words of the narrator were distributed among the actors of the dumb-show and the Globe were erected in Troy, Lydgate's play could be the *Spanish Tragedy* or *Hamlet*.

The persistence of a critical awareness of these principles may be illustrated from a single text, the Prologue to *Henry VIII*, usually said to be by Shakespeare and Fletcher. Who wrote the prologue is unknown, but it does not matter:

> I come no more to make you laugh. Things now
> That bear a weighty and a serious brow,
> Sad, high, and working, full of state and woe,
> Such noble scenes as draw the eye to flow,
> We now present. Those that can pity, here   5
> May (if they think it well) let fall a tear:
> The subject will deserve it. Such as give
> Their money out of hope they may believe,
> May here find truth too. Those that come to see
> Only a show or two and so agree   10
> The play may pass — if they be still and willing,
> I'll undertake may see away their schilling
> Richly in two short hours. Only they
> That come to hear a merry bawdy play,
> A noise of targets, or to see a fellow   15
> In a long motley coat guarded with yellow,
> Will be deceiv'd. For, gentle hearers, know,
> To rank our chosen truth with such a show
> As fool and fight is, beside forfeiting
> Our own brains and the opinion that we bring   20

To make that only true we now intend,
Will leave us never an understanding friend.
Therefore, for goodness sake, as you are known
The first and happiest hearers of the town,
Be sad, as we would make ye. Think ye see   25
The very persons of our noble story
As they were living. Think you see them great,
And follow'd with the general throng, and sweat
Of thousand friends. Then, in a moment, see
How soon this mightiness meets misery.   30
And if you can be merry then, I'll say
A man may weep upon his wedding day.

The basis for discussion is again the sharp distinction of comedy
from tragedy, which is expressed not only in the opening lines
(1-2), but also is introduced with a certain truculence into
the middle where the historical nature of tragedy is affirmed
(13-22, but especially 17-21), and lies behind the turn of
thought in the final lines: for it would be as proper to weep
at the weddings which are the external signs that a comedy has
been concluded:

> Our wooing doth not end like an old play:
> Jack hath not Gill. These ladies' courtesy
> Might well have made our sport a comedy.
> *Love's Labor's Lost*, 5. 2. 883-5

as to be merry at the deaths which conclude a tragedy. For
tragedy is woful. Its subjects are grave and of serious aspect
(2); they are sad, lofty, and have a strong emotional effect
("working," 3); they are noble scenes which evoke tears and
pity (3-7), being full of affairs of state and at the same time
of woe, with the implication that the former qualifies the latter.
Furthermore, the height of the persons and the richness of the
emotional effect are, it is almost implied, proportional
to each other; this is a notion which we shall find made explicit
at the conclusion of *Antony and Cleopatra*:

High events as these
Strike those that make them; and their story is
No less in pity than his glory which
Brought them to be lamented.

5. 2. 363-6

In the final part of the Prologue the spectators are abjured to achieve the full emotional effect intended; they are to be as sad as the authors and actors wish them to be (23-5). They can attain this end (the process is clearly described) by vividly realizing the events on the stage as if they were real, or, indeed, by imputing to them the reality which in fact they have because of the warrant of their historical truth (23-7); in this way the spectators are to achieve the emotional end of historical tragedy, woe or pity — "for sorrow is characteristic of tragedy," as Diomedes says. This effect culminates in the tragic catastrophe, the sudden and violent ("in a moment see," 29) fall from mightiness to misery (27-30).

III

So much for the tradition. But what does Shakespeare himself mean by tragedy? What does the term denote in his works, and with what notions is it associated in context? It denotes primarily violent death, and the notions with which it is associated are the principles of the Donatan tradition. I give now a number of representative passages from Shakespeare's works in which the term *tragedy* or one of its derivatives appears.

A. Talbot in *1 Henry VI*:

Speak, Salisbury; at least, if thou canst speak.
How far'st thou, mirror of all martial men?
One of thy eyes and thy cheek's side struck off?
Accursed tower! Accursed fatal hand
That hath contriv'd this woful tragedy!

1. 4. 73-7

Tragedy is death in battle, the sudden and violent death of a notable person. It is woful. It is brought about by circumstances *(Accursed tower!)* and by a responsible agent *(Accursed fatal hand)*.

B. Gloucester in *2 Henry VI:*

> I know their complot is to have my life;
> And if my death might make this island happy
> And prove the period of their tyranny,
> I would expend it with all willingness.
> But mine is made the prologue to their play;
> For thousands more, that yet suspect no peril,
> Will not conclude their plotted tragedy.
>
> 3. 1. 147-53

Tragedy is the consequence of political intrigue; it involves the destiny of the state; and it concludes with unexpected deaths. But the point of the prophecy in this instance is that here not even holocausts, or tragedy on tragedy, will conclude the plot.

C. Warwick and Queen Margaret over the dead body of Gloucester in *2 Henry VI*—The Queen speaks:

> Then you belike suspect these noblemen
> As guilty of Duke Humphrey's timeless death?

And Warwick:

> Who finds the heifer dead, and bleeding fresh,
> And sees fast-by a butcher with an axe,
> But will suspect 'twas he that made the slaughter?
> Who finds the partridge in the puttock's nest
> But may imagine how the bird was dead,
> Although the kite soar with unbloodied beak?
> Even so suspicious is this tragedy.
>
> 3. 2. 186-94

Tragedy is "timeless death"; that is, untimely, violent, as in *Titus Andronicus* (E, below).

D. Henry VI to Richard in the Tower, *3 Henry VI:*

Ah, kill me with thy weapon, not with words!
My breast can better brook thy dagger's point
Than can my ears that tragic history.

5. 6. 26-8

The tragic history is an account of the death of the young
Prince Edward.

E. *Titus Andronicus*, 2. 3. 265: "timeless tragedy" means
murder, untimely death.

F. *Titus Andronicus*, 4. 1. 45-60: tragedy is rape and
murder.

G. *Richard III.* "Enter Queen with her hair about her
ears, Rivers and Dorset after her."

QUEEN. Ah, who shall hinder me to wail and weep,
To chide my fortune, and torment myself?
I'll join with black despair against my soul
And to myself become an enemy.
DUCHESS OF YORK. What means this scene of rude impatience?
QUEEN. To make an act of tragic violence.
Edward, my lord, thy son, our king, is dead!

2. 2. 34-40

The nature of the act of tragic violence is defined in the preceding speech as sin *(And to myself become an enemy)*, and
specifically as the sin of despair. The characteristic act of
despair is suicide. The act of tragic violence, then, is suicide.

H. Hastings in *Richard III:*

But I shall laugh at this a twelvemonth hence,
That they which brought me in my master's hate,
I live to look upon their tragedy.
Well, Catesby, ere a fortnight make me older,
I'll send some packing that yet think not on't.

3. 2. 57-61

Tragedy is violent unexpected death.

I. *Richard III.* "Enter old Queen Margaret":

So now prosperity begins to mellow
And drop into the rotten mouth of death.
Here in these confines slyly have I lurk'd
To watch the waning of mine enemies.
A dire induction am I witness to,
And will to France, hoping the consequence
Will prove as bitter, black, and tragical.

                                        4. 4. 1-7

The preliminaries are dire — that is, the tragic atmosphere is
one of fear —, and promise by the law of aesthetic congruity
that the consequence will be bitter and black — that is, tragical.
The principle of order that connects preliminaries and consequence is the waning of prosperity: the wheel of Fortune.

   J. *Midsummer's Night's Dream:*

   THESEUS. '. . . very tragical mirth.'
   Merry and tragical? tedious and brief?
   That is hot ice and wondrous strange snow . . . .
   PHILOSTRATE. And tragical, my noble lord, it is;
   For Pyramus therein doth kill himself . . . .
   THESEUS. . . . Marry, if he that writ it had played
   Pyramus and hang'd himself in Thisby's garter,
   it would have been a fine tragedy . . .

                           5.1. 57-9; 66-7; 365-7

Tragedy and comedy are precise contraries. The distinguishing
mark of tragedy is violent death, suicide.

   K. The Archbishop of Canterbury in *Henry V*, 1. 2.
105-6, speaks of "Edward the Black Prince," whose warlike
spirit "on the French ground play'd a tragedy" by slaughtering
the French army.

   L. *Othello*, 5. 2. 363: the representative of the state
speaks of the dead bodies of Desdemona and Othello as "the
tragic loading of this bed."

   M. *The Phoenix and Turtle*, 52: "the tragic scene" is
the death of the phoenix and the dove.

   N. Lucrece in the *Rape of Lucrece:*

"O comfort-killing Night, image of hell!
Dim register and notary of shame!
Black stage for tragedies and murthers fell!
Vast sin-concealing chaos! nurse of blame!
Blind muffled bawd! dark harbour for defame!
Grim cave of death! whisp'ring conspirator
With close-tongu'd treason and the ravisher!"
764-70

This passage constitutes a congeries of the fundamental notions and attitudes associated with the concept of tragedy; its objective content is murder, death, whispering conspiracy, close-tongued treason, rape; it deals in sin — night, its symbol, is the image of Hell, where grace dies (*comfort-killing*) and chaos spreads, for chaos is the issue of sin as order is of grace; tragedy is preoccupied with fame (cf. *Hamlet*, 5. 2. 355-60); its atmosphere is dim, vast (that is, "disordered"), black, blind (that is, "irrational"), dark, grim.

O. The lover in *A Lover's Complaint* is portrayed as a master of insincere rhetoric and capable of expressing all the external signs of the appropriate emotions:

To blush at speeches rank, to weep at woes,
Or to turn white and sound at tragic shows . . .
307-8

The effect of tragedy is fear or terror.

In brief, the tragic atmosphere and the anticipation of the tragic catastrophe is fearful; the catastrophe woful. The process by which the catastrophe comes about involves intrigue, hypocrisy, political conspiracy and treason, acts of sin, and is conducted by responsible agents. These are the connotations of *tragedy*. The denotation is violent, unexpected death — murder, death in battle, suicide. To these is added rape.

This denotation of *tragedy*, however, is not merely Shakespearean; it is generally Elizabethan, as indeed is well known. Death in *Soliman and Perseda*, speaking as a chorus at the beginning of the play, says: "And what are tragedies but acts of death?" (1. 1. 7). And, again, at the conclusion:

> Packe *Loue* and *Fortune*, play in comedies,
> For powerfull Death best fitteth Tragedies.[9]

In the Induction to *A Warning for Fair Women*, which was produced by Shakespeare's company, the characters are Tragedy, History, and Comedy. Tragedy is called "a common executioner," "murther's Beadle," "The common hangman unto Tyranny," and a little later it is remarked:

> Then we shall have a tragedy indeed;
> Pure purple buskin, blood and murther right.
> Induction, 6, 19, 20, 61-2[10]

Finally, Fletcher in the preface to the *Faithful Shepherdess* distinguishes tragi-comedy from tragedy "in respect it wants deaths, which is enough to make it no tragedy. . . ." Hence death is the essential mark — note the technical language of "in respect"—, the defining characteristic.

The tragic fact is death. Even the most natural death has in it a radical violence, for it is a transition from this life to something by definition quite otherwise; and, however much it may be expected, it is in its moment of incidence sudden, for it comes as a thief in the night, you know not the day nor the hour. Hence the characteristics of suddenness and violence which are attached to death in tragedy may be viewed as only artistic heightenings of the essential character of death: the unnaturalness of the tragic event is only pointed and emphasized by the unnatural precipitancy of its accomplishment. If Elizabethan dramas often end in almost indiscriminate butchery, the intention, even if mistaken, is only to make them the more tragic.

That tragedy is death is a conception which will account for a puzzling feature in the history of Elizabethan drama: namely, that we have a number of interesting plays, particularly those traditionally associated with Shakespeare's name, *Arden of Feversham, A Warning for Fair Women,* and the *Yorkshire Tragedy,* in which recent and actual murders are dramatized. These were regarded as tragedies; indeed one of them has the extensive Induction which was quoted from above, in which Tragedy after an argument with History and Comedy introduces the play. Nevertheless, in these plays the usual notion that tragedy involves a notable reversal of prosperity and the fall of a person from high estate to low is little attended to, though not unnoticed, and at the same time the corollary notion that the chief characters should be of princely, or at least of noble, rank is deliberately violated. These are domestic tragedies. The characters involved are usually of what we would call the middle class — they are normally gentlemen. The situation is sordid, not splendid.

It is obvious that such a play, if the principle of decorum is to be observed, must forego the high style appropriate to traditional tragedy. It must forego at the same time the splendor and universality of great events; it must temper its effect to the meanness of its theme. The advantage which such tragedy claims for itself in exchange for the advantages of traditional tragedy is that of unadorned truth — truth in the literal historical sense, and unadorned in the sense of unrhetorical, or lacking the high style. So Tragedy in *A Warning for Fair Women* introduces the sordid story of murder with these remarks:

> My scene is London, native and your own.
> I sigh to think my subject too well-known.
> I am not feigned.

1. 86-8

I am not feigned. Again, the author of *Arden of Feversham,* invoking the age-old commonplace of simple truth as opposed to artful feigning, a commonplace that derives from the early Christian defense of the unliterary character of the New

Testament and from the older classical commonplace of nature and art, concludes the play with these words:

> Gentlemen, we hope you'll pardon this naked Tragedy,
> Wherein no filed points are foisted in
> To make it gracious to the ear or eye;
> For simple truth is gracious enough,
> And needs no other points of glosing stuff.
>
> Epilogue, 14-18[11]

A *naked tragedy* is unrhetorical, lacking in ornament, a tragedy in other than high style. Perhaps one should remark that the play does have a good deal of Kydian ornament in it, but this is beside the point, being only another lamentable example of the gap between profession and practice.

To conclude: if violent death is the distinguishing mark of tragedy, and this seems to be Shakespeare's understanding of the term, it follows 1) that domestic tragedy is a legitimate species since it has the defining characteristic and the associated property of historical truth; 2) that high tragedy will by logical implication involve the fall of princes since the violent death of a high character is such a fall, but that this theme is not logically primitive, but derived; 3) that the tragic attitude will be the attitude toward death; 4) that the tragic effects will be those appropriate to violent death: fear, sorrow, and perhaps wonder at the suddenness and violence; and 5) that the effect of tragedy is consequently not infinitely subtle but quite obvious. On this account the tragedy of *Hamlet* is the holocaust which concludes it, and the tragedy of Hamlet himself is his death.

IV

Wonder

But is wonder a traditional effect of tragedy? Does it appear in the tradition so closely associated with tragic woe that Horatio's *aught of woe or wonder* could be taken as a designation of the tragic effect? Certainly it is not explicit, if present at all, in Donatus or Diomedes. Yet about twenty years before the publication of *Hamlet* Sir Philip Sidney had defined tragedy in the passage already quoted as "stirring the affects of admiration and commiseration."[1] The literal meaning of *admiration* in the Renaissance — it is the meaning of the Latin word *admiratio*—is "wonder." Hence Horatio's phrase is simply a translation from Latin to Germanic diction of Sidney's, with the substitution of the more general and more traditional notion of sorrow for the more special and more Aristotelian notion of pity. Of course, we need not picture Shakespeare as filching his phrase from Sidney, though this is not at all improbable. The question is rather, How did wonder, or admiration, come to be recognized as an effect proper to tragedy, and on what authority was it raised to an equal status with sorrow and fear? On what precedent did Sidney and Shakespeare speak? For surely neither intended to say anything novel on this subject.

I

The precedent is as old as Aristotle's *Poetics*.[2] It is true that in the famous definition of tragedy (1449b24-8) Aristotle speaks only of "incidents arousing pity and fear, wherewith to accomplish its catharsis of such emotions." There is, however, another emotion explicitly associated elsewhere in the *Poetics* with tragic incident and with the tragic catastrophe, and this is wonder or astonishment *(ekplexis, to thaumaston)*.

Three principal texts bear on this point. The first occurs toward the end of the *Poetics*, in the comparison of tragedy and epic:

> The marvellous is certainly required in tragedy. Epic, however, offers more opening for the improbable, the chief factor in the marvellous, because in it the agents are not visibly before us. The scene of the pursuit of Hector would be ridiculous on the stage—the Greeks halting instead of pursuing him, and Achilles shaking his head to stop them; but in the poem the absurdity is overlooked. The marvellous, however, is a cause of pleasure, as is shown by the fact that we all tell a story with additions, in the belief we are doing our hearers a pleasure.
>
> 1460a11-17[3]

The marvellous is certainly required in tragedy. Furthermore, from the example which Aristotle gives of telling a story with additions it is clear that the marvellous derives its value from the point of view of its effect on the audience: wonder, for like begets like.

The point is supported by a later passage, the second principal text, in which Aristotle is discussing the sort of criticisms one may make of the poet's art:

> As to the criticisms relating to the poet's art itself. Any impossibilities there may be in his descriptions of things are faults. But from another point of view they are justifiable, if they serve the end of poetry itself—if (to assume what we have said of that end) they make the effect of either that very portion of the work or some other portion more astounding. The Pursuit of Hector is an instance in point.
>
> 1460b23ff.

That is, impossibilities can be defended on the grounds that they make some portion of the work more astounding. The astounding has therefore a kind of absolute value. As such, it is not merely permissible, but necessary. In fact, the implication of this passage, which occurs in the extended comparison

61

of tragedy and epic, is that epic surpasses tragedy in this respect: you can get away with more of the marvellous in a narration than on the stage, for what seems marvellous when told may seem ridiculous when seen. What is presented on the stage and before our eyes cannot "fly from all humanity." Thus, the element of wonder, which rests upon the improbable, cannot bulk so large or be handled so indiscreetly as in straight narrative, but it cannot be dispensed with. So Aristotle arrives at his canon for the stage: "a likely impossibility is always preferable to an unconvincing possibility" (1460a26-27).

Furthermore, Aristotle posits here that wonder is an end —if it be not the end—of poetry, of which tragedy is a species. Now the end in the Aristotelian scheme is that toward which all things conspire and to which they are subordinated. It will be worth our while, then, to reconcile if possible this passage in which wonder is spoken of as the end of poetry with those others in which is implied that a specific kind of pleasure (involving pity and fear) is the end of tragedy (1448b18; 53a36; 53b11 and 12; 62a16; and 62b13). This passage will furnish the general solution; the third principal text, which will be noticed later, will furnish the specific solution applicable to tragedy.

The relationship of wonder and pleasure is that wonder is pleasurable (1460a17). It is pleasurable in itself. It is pleasurable also in that it is the occasion and motive for learning, as is clear from the famous passage in the *Metaphysics:*

> For it is owing to their wonder that men both now begin and at first began to philosophize. . . . And a man who is puzzled and wonders thinks himself ignorant (whence even the lover of myth is in a sense a lover of Wisdom, for the myth is composed of wonders) . . .
>
> 1. 2. 982b11-19

Furthermore myth, which furnished the material for Greek tragedy, is described as composed of wonders, and the lover of myth is a lover of Wisdom in that he, too, seeks to know.

62

Wonder is the occasion and motive for learning; learning is pleasurable: by this chain are wonder and pleasure connected. This is explained in the *Rhetoric:*

> Again, since learning and wondering are pleasant, it follows that such things as acts of imitation must be pleasant—for instance, painting, sculpture, poetry—and every product of skilful imitation; this latter, even if the object imitated is not itself pleasant; for it is not the object itself which here gives delight; the spectator draws inferences ('That is a so-and-so') and thus learns something fresh. Dramatic turns of fortune and hairbreadth escapes from perils are pleasant, because we feel all such things are wonderful.
>
> 1. 11. 1371b4-12

Wonder and pleasure are the principal effects of art, and consequently of tragedy and the tragic catastrophe; they are its end. The two are correlative, for the one is the motive for inference, the other its natural accompaniment. Furthermore, what we now call aesthetic experience is for Aristotle substantially the experience of inferring. This is clear from the passage just cited, and is reinforced by the well-known passage early in the *Poetics* in which Aristotle analyzes the general origin of poetry. He points out that men, and especially the young, are natural copy-cats and prone to make-believe. This is how they learn. Secondly, he says, "it is natural for all to delight in works of imitation":

> The truth of this second point is shown by experience: though the objects themselves may be painful to see, we delight to view the most realistic representations of them in art, the forms for example of the lowest animals and of dead bodies. The explanation is to be found in a further fact: to be learning something is the greatest of pleasures not only to the philosopher but also the rest of mankind, however small their capacity for it; the reason of the delight in seeing the picture is that one is at the same time learning—gathering the meaning of things, e.g. that the man there is so-and-so; for if one has not seen the thing

before, one's pleasure will not be in the picture as an imitation of it, but will be due to the execution or colouring or some similar cause.

4. 1448b4-19

Wonder, then, is associated with pleasure as the end of poetry, and it is also posited as required in tragedy. But is it specifically associated, as it is in *Hamlet,* with the proper tragic effects of pity and fear? It is, as one would expect, since Aristotle tells us that through pity and fear tragedy attains its proper pleasure (1453b10-11), and pleasure involves wonder. The text, which is the third of the principal texts, reads:

> Tragedy, however, is an imitation not only of a complete action, but also of incidents arousing pity and fear. Such incidents have the very greatest effect on the mind when they occur unexpectedly and at the same time in consequence of one another; there is more of the marvellous in them then than if they happened of themselves or by mere chance. Even matters of chance seem most marvellous if there is an appearance of design as it were in them; as for instance the statue of Mitys at Argos killed the author of Mitys's death by falling down on him when a looker-on at a public spectacle; for incidents like that we think to be not without a meaning. A Plot, therefore, of this sort is necessarily finer than others.

9. 1452a1-11

It is implied again that wonder has an absolute value in itself. Furthermore, the degree of surprise, the amount of the marvellous, in the plot of a tragedy is the measure of the pity and fear it provokes, so that in the strict mathematical sense wonder is a function of pity and fear: $PF = W$.

Two further passages may be cited in this connection. In discussing the kinds of incidents which will produce the tragic pleasure of pity and fear, Aristotle remarks that

> A better situation [than the one previously discussed] is for the deed to be done in ignorance, and the relationship [of the parties

64

involved] discovered afterwards, since there is nothing odious in it, and the Discovery will serve to astound us.

14. 1454a2-4

And later, in analyzing the kinds of Discovery, he remarks:

> The best of all Discoveries, however, is that arising from the incidents themselves, when the great surprise comes about through a probable incident, like that in the *Oedipus* of Sophocles . . .

16. 1455a16-18

In brief, let wonders happen, but make them—at least at the moment of their happening—plausible and convincing. This can best be accomplished by making the tragic incident unexpected, and yet, as soon as it has happened, obviously logical and supported by the situation and the preceding action. The incident is not what we expected, but what, as soon as we see it, we realize that we should have expected. Something of this sort is involved when we understand a person: he acts spontaneously at a crisis in a way we would never have predicted, yet the moment the thing has happened we know that we knew that was the sort of person he was. The point will be clear if we contrast this with our attitude toward the critical actions of those whom we do not understand: their actions simply puzzle us, and the measure of our bewilderment is the measure of our lack of understanding.

There is no need to think all this original with Aristotle: both rhetoric and poetic—the latter in Antiquity is only partially distinguishable from the former—had already a long history by this time. Much of the evidence, it is true, has been lost, and much must be reconstructed by divining earlier features in later texts.[4] But it is clear from the remarks of the rhapsode Ion in Plato's dialogue that fear, pity, and wonder were the commonly recognized effects of the recitation of epic, and particularly of the striking passages: for the whole point of the dialogue, which is simple-mindedly ironic, is that what Ion says should represent common opinion:

65

ION. . . . When I speak of anything piteous, my eyes are filled with tears; when I mention anything fearful or terrible, my hair stands on end with fear and my heart throbs . . .

SOC. And do you not know that you produce the same effects on many of the spectators?

ION. I know it right well, for when I look down from the platform I see them weeping and showing signs of terror and astonishment at my words.

Ion. 535B-C[5]

Nevertheless, most of the subsequent history of the concept of wonder can be derived from the Aristotelian texts. Wonder is, first of all, the natural effect of a marvellous story, and hence of those myths which furnished the plots of ancient tragedy and epic, as well as of those extraordinary events which in later Hellenistic times, as earlier in Herodotus, are narrated in certain types of history and in the marvellous tale. Apuleius, for instance, in the first sentence of the *Metamorphoses* claims that his purpose is to evoke wonder: "I have told these stories," he says, "in this style that you may wonder *(ut mireris)*."

Wonder is, in the second place, the result of a surprising and unexpected turn in events, and is thus intimately involved in the tragic catastrophe and in its proper effect. Furthermore, since in tragedy the turn is toward the worse, the effect of surprise will be inwoven with sorrow or pity as well as astonishment, and the astonishment will take that form which is akin to fear. From this line of thought, though not necessarily from Aristotle, is derived the following passage from a little scrapbook of short treatises by the famous rhetorician Hermogenes of Tarsus, which goes under the title of *How to Speak Effectively:*

Phillipics, dialogue, comedy, tragedy, and the Socratic symposia weave the whole by a kind of double method. . . . The web and woof of tragedy are woe and wonder, as is to be seen both in the tragedies of tragic writers and in those of Homer whom Plato called the father of tragedy and the choregus.[6]

Thirdly, wonder is an end of poetry. This concept is generalized in the Neo-Platonist Plotinus, to whom wonder is an effect of beauty:

> This is the effect that Beauty must ever induce, wonderment and a pleasant astonishment, longing and love and a dread that is pleasurable.
>
> *Enneades,* 1. 6. 4[7]

However, the more restricted view, which we found in Aristotle, that wonder is along with pleasure the end of poetry is a commonplace in later Antiquity; it is chiefly associated with the name of Eratosthenes, the poet-scholar, friend and disciple of Callimachus. We gain our knowledge of his position principally from the criticisms which Strabo levels against it in the *Geography.* "Eratosthenes," he says, "is wrong in his contention that the aim of every poet is to entertain, not to instruct" (1. 1. 10).[8] The argument is long and somewhat tedious. In brief, Strabo holds that the poet either pleases or instructs,— pleases when what he says is false, instructs when what he says is true (1. 2. 3, and 7-9). On this basis the ends of the various branches of composition are distinguished:

> Now the aim of history is truth, . . . the aim of rhetorical composition is vividness, as when Homer introduces men fighting; the aim of myth is to please and excite amazement.
>
> 1. 2. 17

The purpose of myth—that is, of a story—is pleasure and wonder.

Eratosthenes' distinction, as preserved by Strabo, appears also in the historian Polybius. He is criticizing one of his predecessors, Phylarchus, of whom he says:

> Leaving aside the ignoble and womanish character of such a treatment of his subject, let us consider how far it is proper or serviceable to history. A historical author should not try to thrill his readers by such exaggerated pictures, nor should he, like a tragic poet, try to imagine the probable utterances of his

characters or reckon up all the consequences probably incidental to the occurrences with which he deals, but simply record what really happened and what really was said, however commonplace. For the end of tragedy is not the same as that of history but quite the opposite. The tragic poet should amaze and charm his audience for the moment by the verisimilitude of the words he puts into his characters' mouths, but it is the task of the historian to instruct and convince for all time serious students by the truth of the facts and the speeches he narrates, since in the one case it is the probable that takes precedence, even if it be untrue, the purpose being to create illusion in spectators, in the other it is the truth, the purpose being to confer benefit on learners.

2. 56[9]

The passage is intellectually more respectable, of course, than that from Strabo. For Polybius, though he does not exclude—as no one should since literature is a part of life—general ethical judgments ("Leaving aside the ignoble and womanish character of such a treatment of his subject"), is nevertheless capable of discussing literature on its own terms and with reference to its own proper ends ("let us consider how far it is proper and servicable to history"). The end of tragedy is to astonish and please—but not without qualifications, for he points out in the passage that follows this quotation that unless we know the causes of a catastrophe and the course of events which led up to it, it is impossible to feel due indignation or pity. In brief, the effect must be adequately motivated.

Plutarch in his essay on *How a Young Man Should Study Poetry* repeats the commonplace:

> But when poetic art is divorced from the truth, then chiefly it employs variety and diversity. For it is the sudden changes that give to its stories the elements of the emotional, the surprising, and the unexpected, and these are attended by very great astonishment and enjoyment; but sameness is unemotional and prosaic.

7.25[10]

In an earlier passage he applies Eratosthenes' formulation of the end of poetry to a play of Aeschylus:

> But it is patent to everybody that this is a mythical fabrication which has been created to please or astound the hearer.
>
> 7.17

The following passage from the ancient Life of Aeschylus obviously springs from the same context of critical notions: Aeschylus "has few devices for drawing tears" and "uses the spectacle and plot more to strike by the marvellous than to effect artistic illusion."[11]

II

The marvellous is pleasurable. Thus wonder is an end of poetry, or it is with pleasure the end of poetry. Hence it would obviously be involved in the effect of any particular kind. It is, however, associated with the specific, rather than with the generic, effect of tragedy even in Aristotle, since the specific effects of pity and fear are most truly effective when they also involve wonder. Indeed, the marvellous is required in tragedy. Consequently, it becomes traditional to distinguish the purpose of fiction, especially of epic and tragedy, from that of history and of rhetoric on these grounds: fiction aims at wonder and pleasure; history at truth and instruction; rhetoric at vividness and persuasion. But, of course, these lines of distinction were not fixed and unalterable in Antiquity, since the subjects of the distinctions were not simple. Poetry and rhetoric had a great deal in common; fiction commonly involved history, and history fiction. Furthermore, from the time of Aristotle poetry was often identified with fiction, and the mythical was a characteristic property. Thus, the end of poetry was often said to be pleasure and instruction, as in Horace and Strabo, and its methods were usually rhetorical.

However, wonder is not only an effect of a story or of a

subject matter, it is also an effect of language and of style. It is precisely the effect of characteristically poetic, or tragic, style, as opposed to the plain straightforward style proper to prose and to dialectic. For the fundamental distinction which prevails in Antiquity and informs the traditional theory of the three (or four) styles is the distinction in diction between the unornamented language native to prose and the unusual, figurative, ornamented language of poetry, and especially of tragedy. The distinction remained current even though poetry appropriated the language of prose, as in the later tragedians, and prose in the rhetorical tradition of Gorgias appropriated the language of poetry (Aristotle, *Rhet.* 3. 1. 1404a20-34; Strabo, 1. 2. 6). The point is made clear by Aristotle in the *Rhetoric.* The effect of poetic diction is wonder.

> People do not feel toward strangers as they do towards their own countrymen, and the same thing is true of their feeling for language. It is therefore well to give everyday speech an unfamiliar air: wonder is a characteristic of things off the beaten track, and the wonderful is pleasant. In verse such effects are common, and there they are fitting; the persons and things there spoken of are comparatively remote from ordinary life. In prose passages they are far less often fitting because the subject-matter is less exalted.

> 3. 2. 1404b8-15[12]

The later theory on the subject derives partly from such passages as this, probably by way of Theophrastus' work on style, and partly no doubt from Sophistic theory as developed by Gorgias among others. (Diodorus, 12. 53; Gorgias, *Helena,* 9.) It seems to have been based, at least originally, upon a distinction between style which employs plain language and to the point, whose aim is merely truth, and whose concern is simply with content *(rem tene, verba secuntur),* and a style cultivated as such. The former uses proper expressions only; the latter intermingles figurative. Its aim is to move, to convince, to please; its concern is with the effect on the audience. The former is the style of dialectic and, in general, of philosophy; and the latter is the style of poetry and of rhetoric. So Theophrastus in a passage preserved in one of the later commentaries on Aristotle's logic:

> Language is divided into two types, according to the philosopher Theophrastus, the one having reference to the hearers, the other to the matter concerning which the speaker aims to convince his audience. To the division with reference to the hearers belong poetry and rhetoric. Therefore its function is to choose the more stately words, and not those which are common or vulgar, and to interweave them with each other harmoniously, to the end that, by means of them and the effects which result from the employment of them, such as vividness, sweetness and other qualities of style, together with studied expansion and contraction, all employed at the suitable moment, the listener shall be charmed and astonished and, with respect to intellectual persuasion, overmastered. The division looking to the matter will be the especial concern of the philosopher, refuting the false and setting forth the true.[13]

The effect of astonishment or wonder is the natural correlative of unusual diction, as it is of the unusual event. The proper word satisfies by its exactness; the unusual pleases or displeases by its startling effect. Upon this basis, which though obvious is not unimportant, together with the doctrine of the appropriateness of style to subject, rests the whole later theory of the kinds and characters of style in all its elaboration. Hence, the theorists will ascribe to any style which is noticeable as such the quality of wonder. That style which is elaborated for the purpose of charm or pleasure—the *genus floridum*—will evoke the kind of pleasant wonder that the marvellous story does, and will be appropriate to such subjects: for instance, the Milesian style of Apuleius, for the effect of wonder is ascribed in the passage cited above not only to the subject matter but also to the style. The high style, the forceful, the grand—the style

71

of Demosthenes and of Aeschylus—will evoke that wonder which is akin to fear, and will be especially appropriate to tragedy. Yet wonder may be on a lesser scale than this: it corresponds to the displacement, large or small, that initiates internal movement: with respect to the intellect, inference, the processes of logic, and learning; with respect to the irrational part of the soul, feeling and emotion. Hence style can evoke emotion in the audience, and at the same time by the law of decorum the degree of unusual diction should be proportionate to the height and intensity of the feeling inherent in the subject-matter. Again, to wonder at style is to regard it highly, to approve of it, to admire in the modern sense, but this attitude, though not unaccompanied by feeling, nevertheless implies no specific shade of emotional coloring.

This much may serve to introduce the following citations in which is exhibited the continuity in antiquity of the Peripatetic and Sophistic tradition that wonder is an effect of style, and especially of the high style appropriate to tragedy. The treatise on style by Demetrius (probably first century A. D.) is clearly in this tradition. He cites a line of Homer in which a figurative shift in construction elevates the style, and contrasts this with the ordinary way of saying the same thing. "But everything ordinary is trivial," he says, "and so fails to attain wonder" (59-60). Again, to take a longer quotation:

> The sayings of Demades, too, possess power, although their expression sounds peculiar and unusual. Their power arises partly from their significance and partly from their allegorical form and lastly from their exaggerated character.

> This is an example: "Alexander is not dead, Athenians. If he were, the whole world would smell the corpse." The use of the word "smell" for "perceive" involves both allegory and exaggeration. The fact that the world perceived it signifies Alexander's strength, and at the same time the sentence has an effect of astonishment which is due to a combination of three causes.

Everything that astonishes is powerful, because it creates fear.
282-3[14]

The rhetorical concept of wonder is the subject of the famous treatise on elevated style *(On the Sublime)*, which has been ascribed to Longinus. The subject is announced in the opening chapter. The author premises that the eminence and renown of great writers, both in prose and in verse, is derived from distinction in language (1. 3). The effect of such distinction he conceives of in the traditional way—the doctrine is precisely that of the passage cited above from Theophrastus — as astonishment, which overpowers the hearer and puts him in a state of transport. This effect is differentiated from that of persuasion, and incidentally of pleasure, on the grounds that this is irresistible while persuasion for the most part involves voluntary assent, and secondly that this is a matter of detail and that of the work as a whole (1. 4).

In this way the differences which Eratosthenes, Polybius, and Strabo, among others, had established between the various kinds of literary works are here applied in the context of rhetorical theory to single out the special effect of certain details in a work. The analysis gets sometimes a little complicated. Thus, in discussing the kind of image in which out of an inspired passion the writer thinks he sees what he is describing and makes his hearer see it—a well-known rhetorical device in Antiquity — Longinus distinguishes between the purpose of such images in oratory and in the poets. In poetry the end is astonishment; in prose vividness; though both alike seek to stir up excitement (15. 36). But the poetic image tends to be fabulous, exaggerated, and to go beyond what is believable, whereas the virtue of imagery in prose is always its reality and truth (15. 40). Nevertheless, imagery in prose can exceed persuasion and attain astonishment, combining vigor and passion with argument and fact so that the hearer is not merely persuaded but actually enslaved, for the stronger effect of wonder will absorb the weaker of persuasion (15. 41).[15]

The notion also appears, as we might expect, in the Latin authors. Cicero, for example, in the teacher-pupil dialogue on the *Classification of Oratory* associates wonder with ornate or figurative diction, and hence with the charming style *(genus suave)*. He points out that style will be charming if something unusual, original, or novel is said — he is thinking of phrasing —, "for anything wonderful pleases" (22). Again, a charming account is one that has causes of wonder, suspense, and emotional outcomes, along with interpolated emotional passages, dialogues, sorrow, anger, fear, joy, and desire (32). Cicero is here speaking of those expositions of events which form part of a speech, but the description could easily apply to a play, and particularly to such as the *Winter's Tale* or to many of Beaumont and Fletcher. In another passage he says that in developing a subject in the decorative style we should take up those aspects that produce suspense, wonder, and delight (58). Finally, he points out in an extended passage that in epideictic speeches, whose chief purpose is to please and entertain an audience, the speaker should make use of striking phrases, which have a great deal of charm; that is, he should use coined words, archaisms, and metaphors, and in constructing the phrase one should echo another by similarity of rhythm and ending, thus giving doublets and a verbal rhythm, not sounding like verse yet satisfying the ear with an appropriate harmony. But the ornament should not be merely verbal; there should also be in the matter a good deal of what is wonderful and unexpected, things foreshadowed by portents, prodigies, and oracles, and what seems to the man to whom this happens to be the result of divine intervention or of fate. For the feeling of suspense in the audience, and wonder, and the unexpected outcome always give a certain pleasure in the hearing (72-3).[16] What is described here is represented in Elizabethan times by Lyly's *Euphues,* and all its progeny in the Elizabethan drama. Wonder is an effect both of style and of subject.

The doctrine of Antiquity on wonder is summed up and transmitted to posterity by Quintilian:

. . . those words are the most to be commended which express our thoughts best, and produce the impression which we desire on the minds of the judges. Such words undoubtedly must make a speech both worthy of admiration and productive of pleasure; but not of that kind of *admiration* with which we wonder at monsters; or of that kind of *pleasure* which is attended with unnatural gratification, but such as is compatible with true merit and worth.

8. *Pr.* 32-3

It was the sublimity, magnificence, splendour, and dignity of his [Cicero's] eloquence, that drew forth that thunder of approbation. No such extraordinary commendation would have attended on the speaker, if his speech had been of an everyday character, and similar to ordinary speeches. I even believe that his audience were insensible of what they were doing, and that they gave their applause neither voluntarily nor with an exercise of judgment, but that, being carried away by enthusiasm, and unconscious of the place in which they stood, they burst forth instinctively into such transports of delight.

But this grace of style may contribute in no small degree to the success of a cause; for those who listen with pleasure are both more attentive and more ready to believe; they are very frequently captivated with pleasure, and sometimes hurried away in admiration. Thus the glitter of a sword strikes something of terror into the eyes, and thunder storms themselves would not alarm us so much as they do if it were their force only, and not also their flame, that was dreaded. Cicero, accordingly, in one of his letters to Brutus, makes with good reason the following remark: *That eloquence which excites no wonder, I account as nothing.* Aristotle, also, thinks that to excite wonder should be one of our greatest objects.

8. 3. 2-6[17]

75

So much for Antiquity. It will be sufficient now to establish the continuity of the tradition in the Middle Ages, and later in the Renaissance. The effect of wonder will be a familiar notion to any Christian since it is frequently noted in the New Testament as the effect of the words and works of Christ:

And the disciples were astonished at his words. . .

Mt. 13. 54

And straightway the damsel arose and walked, for she was of the age of twelve years. And they were astonished with a great astonishment.

Mk. 5.42

Wonder, of course, is the natural effect of miracles, real or apparent. St. Augustine makes the point in the text which furnishes the standard definition for medieval theology: "I call a miracle anything great and difficult or unusual that happens beyond the expectation or ability of the man who wonders at it" *(De Utilitate Credendi, 16. 34)*.[18] And St. Thomas, in turn, integrates the Augustinian definition with the Aristotelian. In the *Summa* he takes up the question, "Whether everything that God does outside of the natural order is miraculous?" He cites an authoritative text from St. Augustine: "When God does anything contrary to the course and custom of nature as we know it, we call it a miracle." For the term is indeed derived from the word for wonder, and wonder arises whenever an effect is manifest and its cause hidden, as Aristotle says in the *Metaphysics*. Consequently, what is wonderful to one man may not be wonderful to another, but a miracle is fully wonderful since it has a cause absolutely hidden from all, namely, God *(ST* 1. 105.7).

The marvellous event, and so the marvellous story, provokes wonder. The explicit recognition of this effect is common throughout the literature of the Middle Ages, and has behind it a tradition derived from Christian dogma. Thus the German *Niebelungenlied* of the twelfth century begins by promising us that now we will hear a wonder told, and so likewise in countless romances.

But with the recovery of the Aristotelian writings in the twelfth and thirteenth centuries, the concept of wonder as the end of poetry again enters firmly into the tradition under the authority of Aristotle and in association with most of the other elements in the tradition which were distinguished in the preceding sections of this essay. One of the most interesting texts is to be found in the works of St. Albert the Great, the teacher of Thomas Aquinas. It occurs in Albert's *Commentary on the Metaphysics of Aristotle;* I shall cite it at length:

Ch. 6: *In which it is shown that philosophy is a speculative, not a practical, science.*

That philosophy is speculative, not practical, is clear from the motive that first moved men to philosophize. For everyone who has philosophized, now or in the past, has been motivated only by wonder. Now, wonder is defined as a constriction and suspension of the heart caused by amazement at the sensible appearance of something so portentous, great, and unusual, that the heart suffers a systole. Hence wonder is something like fear in its effect on the heart. This effect of wonder, then, this constriction and systole of the heart, springs from an unfulfilled but felt desire to know the cause of that which appears portentous and unusual: so it was in the beginning when men, up to that time unskilled, began to philosophize—they marvelled at certain difficulties, which were, as a matter of fact, fairly easy to solve. The Pythagoreans, for example, were concerned with the theory of number, with even and odd numbers, with complete, increasing, and diminished number. Then men advanced bit by bit in learning and, becoming more proficient, raised graver questions whose causes were not easy to see: such as the changes of the moon with respect to mansions, accessions, and eclipses, or questions about the sun and the stars. . . . In like fashion they advanced in Physics, and began to wonder about generation in general, asking whether the universe was created or given.

Now the man who is puzzled and wonders apparently does not know. Hence wonder is the movement of the man who does not know on his way to finding out, to get at the bottom of that at which he wonders and to determine its cause. A token in proof is that the famous Philomithes according to this way of looking at the matter is a Philosopher, for he constructed his stories out of wonderful events. I hold that Philomithes was a poet who loved to fashion stories: for *mithes,* with the first syllable long, is the word for stories, and *Philomithes,* then, means a lover of stories, if you make the penultimate syllable long. Thus Aristotle shows in that branch of logic which is called poetic that the poet fashions his story for the purpose of exciting wonder, and that the further effect of wonder is to excite inquiry. Such is the origin of philosophy, as Plato shows with respect to the stories of Phaeton and Deucalion. The single purpose of these stories is to excite one to wonder at the causes of the two deluges of fire and of water (which issued from the circut of wandering stars), so that through wonder the cause would be looked for, and the truth discovered.

Hence poetry offers a method of philosophizing, just as do the other sciences of logic. But the other sciences or branches of logic offer a method of proving a proposition by reasoning, that is, by conclusive or probable argument; poetry, however, offers no method of proof but rather a method of wonder by which we are incited to inquiry. Therefore, though poetry is a subdivision of grammar with respect to prosody, with respect to its purpose it is one of the branches of logic.

To get back to the point: we define the man who wonders as one who is in suspense as to the cause, the knowledge of which would make him know instead of wonder. . . .

In I Met., Tr. 2,ch. 6[19]

The poet Philomithes, of course, is a character that grew from a misreading of the Greek text in the passage in which Aristotle states that "the lover of myth *(philomuthos)* is in a sense a lover of Wisdom, for the myth is composed of wonders" *(Metaphysics,* 1. 2. 982b18-9). But he is a charming character, and he makes the point. The end of poetry is wonder, and the end of wonder is to excite inquiry; thus poetry is a branch of logic with respect to its purpose, and distinguished from other branches in that they offer methods of proof but poetry offers a method of motivation. Its physiological effect is similar to that of fear.

St. Thomas holds substantially the same position, and cites Aristotle in the *Poetics* to the same effect. He is discussing the causes of pleasure, and comes finally to the question, Does wonder cause pleasure? He first takes up the objections:

Apparently it doesn't 1) since wonder is a property of ignorance, and ignorance is not pleasurable, but rather knowledge. 2) Furthermore, wonder is the beginning of wisdom, being as it were a way of looking for the truth, as is said in the *Metaphysics,* 1, 2. But it is more pleasurable to contemplate what is already known than to inquire into the unknown, as Aristotle says in the *Ethics* X, 7. (1177a23ff.), since the latter offers difficulties and impediments, but the former does not, and pleasure arises from unimpeded operation. Therefore wonder is not a cause of pleasure, but rather a hinderance. 3) Furthermore, everyone delights in what he is used to; hence the operation of habits acquired through daily use is pleasurable. But what one is used to is not wonderful, as Augustine says (at the beginning of *In Joan.,* tr. 24). Therefore wonder is precisely not a cause of pleasure.

But to the contrary is the text of Aristotle (Rhet. 1. 11. 1371a31): *wonder is a cause of pleasure.*

My position is that to attain anything one feels a want of is pleasurable; and the measure of anyone's desire for something he loves is the measure of his pleasure in attaining it. Indeed, in the very augmentation of desire there is an augmentation of pleasure, in that there arises a hope of what is loved, and desire itself is pleasurable in its aspect of hope. But wonder is a kind of desire for knowledge. The situation arises when one sees an effect and does not know its cause, or when the cause of the particular effect is one that exceeds his power of understanding. Hence wonder is a cause of pleasure in so far as there is annexed the hope of attaining understanding of that which one wants to know.

For this reason, everything wonderful is pleasurable: for example, anything that is infrequent, as well as any representation of things, even of those that are not in themselves pleasant. For the soul delights in comparing one thing with another, since this is a proper and connatural activity of reason, as Aristotle says in his *Poetics* (4. 1448b13ff.). And for this reason even to be released from great danger is quite pleasurable, as is said in the *Rhetoric* (1.11.1371b10ff.).

As to the first objection, wonder is not pleasurable in so far as it involves ignorance, but in so far as it involves learning the cause, and learning something new: namely, that such-and-such is such-and-such, though we had not thought it was.

As to the second objection, there are two kinds of pleasure: acquiescence in the Good, and awareness of such acquiescence. With respect to the former, since it is a more complete experience to contemplate known truth than to inquire into the unknown, the contemplation of things known is in itself more pleasurable than inquiry into things unknown; nevertheless, it sometimes happens that, with respect to our awareness of experience, inquiry is more pleasurable in that it has more drive and springs from a greater desire. For desire is especially aroused by the awareness of ignorance, and consequently a man takes the greatest pleasure in those things which he discovers for himself or learns from the ground up.

As to the third objection, doing what we are used to is pleasurable in so far as it is in a way natural to us. Still, on the other hand, what is unusual can be pleasurable, either with respect to the process of learning, since our desire for knowledge is proportional to the marvellousness of the subject, or with respect to the actual doing, since the mind is strongly impelled by desire to that which is felt intensely because of its novelty. But an activity, the more full it is, the greater the pleasure it causes.   1-2. 32. 8[20]

Wonder is also a species of fear, as the Damascene teaches. To the objection that wonder and amazement *(admiratio et stupor)* are not species of fear, since fear refers only to evil, and wonder and amazement refer to the unusual, whether good or evil; and again, to the further objection that philosophers are moved by wonder to inquire into the truth, whereas fear does not move one to investigate but rather to run from the scene of investigation; Thomas answers that the authority of the Damascene and of Gregory of Nyassa is sufficient to establish the point. He then solves the objections by dividing the six traditional species of fear into three whose source is internal and three whose source is external — wonder *(admiratio)*, which arises when one contemplates some great evil whose issue he cannot see; amazement *(stupor)*, which arises when one contemplates some unaccustomed evil, for it will seem to be great because it is unaccustomed; shocked surprise *(agonia)*, which arises from the unforeseen. Hence to the former objection Thomas answers that only that wonder and amazement which arises from the contemplation of evil is a species of fear; to the latter objection he answers that a man who wonders does fear at the moment to give a judgment, fearing that he will fail, but that he looks into the matter in the future; the amazed man, however, fears both now and in the future; hence wonder is the beginning of philosophizing, but amazement an impediment to it *(ST*, 1-2. 41. 4).

IV

Whatever appears in the scholastic philosophers and at the same time in Aristotle, as well as in Cicero and Quintillian, is likely to appear anywhere in Renaissance literature. It will be commonplace. Thus the rhetorical tradition is gathered up, assimilated, and integrated into a consistent structure in Pontanus' dialogue on poetry (*Actius*, about 1500). There the end of poetry is said to be "to speak well and appropriately so as to attain wonder," and this is later corrected by one of the speakers into the form, "to speak exceptionally well," so as to distinguish the poet from the orator who also must speak well and appropriately. The wonder referred to is conceived under two aspects: it is admiration, in the modern sense, for the eloquence of the poet himself, who from this source derives his fame and glory; at the same time, it is the emotion of wonder in the audience. The poet moves wonder not only by sublime words, but also by his subject matter, and since truth alone cannot guarantee this he shades truth with fiction and myth. Nor is wonder only the effect of the grave and serious; it is also the effect of the pleasant and delightful. And in speaking so sweetly, sublimely, and marvellously, the poet teaches others to speak well, so that every literary form derives from poetry.[21]

The same line of thought is developed in Fracastoro's dialogue *Navagero* (published 1555), in which the emphasis, however, is laid on the final remark, and poetry is distinguished from all other forms in that it is the master-art of eloquence. For, though poetry excites wonder, this is not its exclusive characteristic since wonder is also the effect of oratory and history: "Who can read Cicero himself without wonder?"[22]

The idea is common throughout the Renaissance. Minturno, who is in the same line of tradition as Pontanus and Fracastoro, begins his dialogue on the poet, *De Poeta* (1559), with the statement that "no one can be called a poet who does not excel in the power of arousing wonder." Minturno, however, goes beyond the rhetorical tradition, making a good deal of Aristotle's *Poetics* which had lately been translated, paraphrased, and expounded by a good many of his fellow-countrymen. Thus he introduces the notions of wonder and pleasure in connection with tragedy:

82

The poet does not deal with what does not please, nor does he move the emotions without delight. Rather, excited by the force of language and the weight of his ideas he rouses, attracts, and moves the audience intensely to the point of wonder—either through fear or pity, or both.[23]

In fact, the idea of wonder is so commonplace in the Renaissance it would be surprising not to find it in Sidney or in Shakespeare. Hence, to establish the availability of the idea, I will only add to these citations and that from Sidney's *Defense* the following passages from Spenser.

A. Wonder is the effect of theological discourse, being, of course, the highest subject-matter and hence affording by its very nature the highest eloquence; as such, however, it is an effect of subject, not of style:

> And that her sacred Booke, with blood ywritt,
> That none could reade, except she did them teach,
> She unto him disclosed every whitt,
> And heavenly documents thereout did preach,
> That weaker witt of man could never reach,
> Of God, of grace, of justice, of free will,
> That wonder was to heare her goodly speach:
> For she was hable with her wordes to kill
> And rayse againe to life the hart that she did thrill.
>
> *Faerie Queene*, 1. 10. 19

Compare Milton's *Paradise Lost:* At Raphael's speech Adam,

> with his consorted Eve,
> The story heard attentive, and was filled
> With admiration and deep muse, to hear
> Of things so high and strange . . .
>
> 7. 50-3

B. The palmer finds good Guyon, "slumbering fast, in senseles dreame":

> Whom when the palmer saw, abasht he was
> Through fear and wonder, that he nought could say . . .
>
> *F. Q.*, 2. 8. 7. 1-2

83

Fear and wonder is the effect of apparent unexpected death.

C. Ruth (that is, pity or woe) and wonder is the effect on the bystanders at a mortal combat:

> With that they both together fiercely met,
> As if that each ment other to devoure;
> And with their axes both so sorely bet,
> That neither plate nor mayle, whereas their power
> They felt, could once sustaine the hideous stowre,
> But rived were like rotton wood a sunder,
> Whilest through their rifts the ruddie bloud did showre,
> And fire did flash, like lightning after thunder,
> That fild the lookers on attonce with ruth and wonder.
>
> *F. Q.*, 4. 3. 15

Attonce means "both."

D. The following marvellous events quite properly provoke great wonder of a kind akin to fear, as do the prodigies of Nature:

> Then forth he brought his snowy Florimele,
> Whom Trompart had in keeping there beside,
> Covered from peoples gazement with a vele.
> Whom when discovered they had throughly eide,
> With great amazement they were stupefide;
> And said, that surely Florimell it was,
> Or if it were not Florimell so tride,
> That Florimell her selfe she then did pas.
> So feeble skill of perfect things the vulgar has.
>
> Which when as Marinell beheld likewise,
> He was therewith exceedingly dismayd;
> Ne wist he what to thinke, or to devise,
> But, like as one whom feends had made affrayd,
> He long astonisht stood, ne ought he sayd,
> Ne ought he did, but with fast fixed eies
> He gazed still upon that snowy mayd;
> Whom ever as he did the more avize,
> The more to be true Florimell he did surmize.

As when two sunnes appeare in the azure skye,
Mounted in Phoebus charet fierie bright,
Both darting forth faire beames to each mans eye,
And both adorn'd with lampes of flaming light,
All that behold so strange prodigious sight,
Not knowing Natures worke, nor what to weene,
Are rapt with wonder and with rare affright:
So stood Sir Marinell, when he had seene
The semblant of this false by his faire beauties queene.
                              F. Q., 5. 3. 17-19

Then Artegall steps forth and says this " 'is not (I wager) Florimell at all' . . . For proof whereof he bad them Florimell forth
call."

Then did he set her by that snowy one,
Like the true saint beside the image set,
Of both their beauties to make paragone,
And triall, whether should the honor get.
Streight way so soone as both together met,
Th' enchanted damzell vanisht into nought:
Her snowy substance melted as with heat,
Ne of that goodly hew remayned ought,
But th' emptie girdle, which about her waste was wrought.

As when the daughter of Thaumantes faire
Hath in a watry cloud displayed wide
Her goodly bow, which paints the liquid ayre;
That all men wonder at her colours pride;
All suddenly, ere one can looke aside,
The glorious picture vanisheth away,
Ne any token doth thereof abide:
So did this ladies goodly forme decay,
And into nothing goe, ere one could it bewray.

Which when as all that present were beheld,
They stricken were with great astonishment,
And their faint harts with senselesse horrour queld,
To see the thing, that seem'd so excellent,

So stolen from their fancies wonderment:
That what of it became none understood.
And Braggadochio selfe with dreriment
So daunted was, in his despeyring mood,
That like a lifelesse corse immoveable he stood.

F. Q., 5. 3. 24-6

E. "Calidore sees young Tristram slay / A proud discourteous knight":

Which when he saw, his hart was inly child
With great amazement, and his thought with wonder fild.

F. Q., 6. 2. Argum. and 4. 8-9

F. In *The Ruines of Time*:

Before mine eyes strange sights presented were,
Like tragicke pageants seeming to appeare.

489-90

Then follows a series of visions in which a gold image, a stately tower, a pleasant paradise, a giant, a gold bridge over the sea, and two white bears successively fall to ruin:

Much was I troubled in my heavie spright,
At sight of these sad spectacles forepast,
That all my senses were bereaved quight,
And I in minde remained sore agast,
Distraught twixt feare and pitie; when at last
I heard a voyce, which loudly to me called,
That with the suddein shrill I was appalled.

'Behold,' said it, 'and by ensample see,
That all is vanitie and griefe of minde,
No other comfort in this world can be,
But hope of heaven, and heart to God inclinde;
For all the rest must needs be left behinde.'

575-86

The effect of these tragic pageants is wonder ("That all my

senses were bereaved quight") which suspends and mediates between fear and pity. The ultimate effect is to teach the rejection of this life.

v

Certainly the aesthetic effect of wonder was a notion easily available to Shakespeare. But if Horatio's *aught of woe or wonder* is to be taken as aesthetically significant, it must be shown not only that Shakespeare could have been but also that he was aware of the tradition. Does Shakespeare use the notion of wonder, and the synonymous *amazement, astonishment,* and *to be struck senseless,* in any other contexts than this one in Hamlet? He does. In fact, he uses almost the full range of meanings which are to be found in the tradition.

Wonder is the effect of such an incident, conventional to tragedy, as the appearance of the Ghost in *Hamlet* and the recognition of his likeness to the dead King:

> BERNARDO. Looks it not like the King? Mark it, Horatio.
> HORATIO. Most like. It harrows me with fear and wonder.
> 1. 1. 43-4

The appearance is regarded by Horatio (1. 1. 113-25) as of the same nature as those signs and portents, those foreshadowings of tragic consequences, which preceded the death of Caesar. Indeed, such "precurse of fierce events," such "harbingers preceding still the fates / And prologue to the omen coming on" have precisely the same effect upon Casca in the play of *Julius Caesar:*

> CASCA. It is the part of men to fear and tremble
> When the most mighty gods by tokens send
> Such dreadful heralds to astonish us.

To which Cassius replies;

> . . . You look pale, and gaze
> And put on fear, and cast yourself in wonder,
> To see the strange impatience of the heavens. . . .
> 1. 3. 54-6 and 59-61

Wonder, then, is an emotion which is a kind of fear and is produced by striking and supernatural events. But, truly, one doesn't have to see the ghost in order to experience the effect: the Ghost in the closet scene is invisible to Hamlet's mother, yet the effect on her of Hamlet's apparently wild actions, his holding discourse with the incorporeal air, and the communicated effect of his manifest fear and wonder—

> Forth at your eyes your spirits wildly peep;
> And, as the sleeping soldiers in th' alarm,
> Your bedded hairs, like life in excrements,
> Start up and stand an end. —

are characterized by the Ghost himself as an effect of amazement:

> But look, amazement on thy mother sits.
> 3. 4. 119-22, 112

Wonder is also an effect of the plot as a whole, and not merely of incident. Theseus and Hippolyta in *Midsummer Night's Dream* discuss the events of the same play, the plot of the criss-crossing lovers, from the point of view of literary criticism (the passage contains the famous remarks on "the poet's eye in a fine frenzy rolling"):

> HIPPOLYTA. 'Tis strange, my Theseus, that these lovers speak of.
> THESEUS. More strange than true. . . .
> HIPPOLYTA. But all the story of the night told over,
> And all their minds transfigur'd so together,
> More witnesseth than fancy's images
> And grows to something of great constancy;
> But howsoever, strange and admirable.
> 5. 1. 1-2 and 23-27

The plot, whether true or not, is certainly strange and wonderful *(admirable)*.

Wonder, however, is especially the effect of the denouement of those plays which the literary historian calls romances, especially if they conclude with a marvellous and surprising turn of events. Thus, in the *Winter's Tale* the "discovery" that Perdita is the King's daughter is described by the First Gentlemen as "a little amazedness." He goes on:

> . . . but the changes I perceived in the King and Camillo were very notes of admiration. They seem'd almost, with staring on one another, to tear the cases of their eyes. There was speech in their dumbness, language in their very gesture. They look'd as they had heard of a world ransom'd, or one destroyed. A notable passion of wonder appeared in them; but the wisest beholder that knew no more but seeing, could not say if th' importance were joy or sorrow; but in the extremity of the one it must needs be.
>
> 5. 2. 5-6, 9-21

He, however, had been commanded out of the chamber, and did not have the full story; hence, so far as he was concerned, it was "a little amazedness," provoked mainly by the wonder of the King and Camillo. The Second Gentleman, who now enters, is better informed and tells us:

> Such a deal of wonder is broken out within this hour that balladmakers cannot be able to express it.
>
> 5. 2. 25-7

Wonder, then, is the effect of the surprising and the marvellous; it is an extremity of feeling, and hence may be either joy or sorrow, fear or rapture. It is, if not the actual effect of such plots as the *Winter's Tale,* at least the effect aimed at. Thus Paulina, the mistress of ceremonies in the following scene, remarks as she discloses Hermione standing like a statue:

> I like your silence; it the more shows off
> Your wonder.
>
> 5. 3. 21-2

And the disclosure certainly has such an effect on Perdita; witness the King's speech:

89

> O royal piece,
> There's magic in thy majesty, which has. . .
> From thy admiring daughter took the spirits,
> Standing like stone with thee!
> 5. 3. 38-9, 41-2

But there is more wonder still! Paulina warns her audience that they remain at their own risk:

> Quit presently the chapel, or resolve you
> For more amazement.
> 5. 3. 86-7

And when the King commands, "No foot shall stir," she speaks to the statue:

> 'Tis time; descend; be stone no more; approach;
> Strike all that look upon with marvel.
> 5. 3. 98-100

So, if the reader finds the events of the play improbable, that is the point. They are intended to be improbable. The effect aimed at is pleasurable wonder.

In comparable circumstances, at the denouement of the serious plot of *Much Ado*, when Hero appears alive, the Friar says:

> All this amazement can I qualify . . .
> Meantime let wonder seem familiar. . .
> 5. 4. 67 and 70

Wonder, then, is associated not only with extreme fear but also with extreme joy, and is marked by silence and immobility. It is the shocked limit of feeling. Hence, Descartes a few years later chose wonder as the first, and indeed the principal, passion of the soul (*Les Passions du Ame*, 2. 53; 69-78).

It is easy to understand that the marvellous is intended to be wonderful, whether in fact the reader finds it so or not. But tragedy should not so fly from all probability. In what way, then, does Shakespearean tragedy in general, and the tragic

90

catastrophe in particular, admit of the effect of wonder? I have already shown how certain conventional tragic incidents and certain conventional appurtenances of tragic atmosphere involve fear and wonder. But a tragedy is not merely a spectacle and a plot, it is also something written and spoken; it is in large measure a series of declamations. This is obviously true of Elizabethan tragedy and of Shakespearean.

In fact, the revolution in the English theatre of the 1580's out of which came the great plays of the succeeding decades consisted largely in the introduction of an adequate rhetoric. Nashe, for example, characterizes the pre-Shakespearean *Hamlet* and related plays as "handfuls of tragical speeches." Again, it is Greene's dying complaint against the companies of actors that he has been "of them forsaken," "those puppets . . . that spake from our mouths, those antics garnished in our colors" — that is, in our colors of rhetoric. It is his complaint against Shakespeare himself that he "supposes he is as well able to bombast out a blank verse as the best of" Greene's companions.[24] Marlowe's *Tamburlaine, Parts I* and *II* are, according to his printer, "tragical discourses"; and Marlowe himself enunciated in the prologue to *Tamburlaine I,* in those lines which constitute the charter of the greater Elizabethan tragedies, the rhetorical principle of high style in tragedy and its concomitant effect of wonder or astonishment:

> From jigging veins of rhyming mother wits
> And such conceits as clownage keeps in pay,
> We'll lead you to the stately tent of war
> Where you shall hear the Scythian Tamburlaine
> Threatening the world with high astounding terms
> And scourging kingdoms with his conquering sword.
> View but his picture in this tragic glass,
> And then applaud his fortunes as you please.

Though these lines have often been quoted, they are

worth noticing again, for they are packed with critical doctrine. They are a manifesto. The first two lines constitute an explicit rejection of the old theatrical tradition of the fourteener with its rhyme and its marked regularity of metre *(jigging veins)*; of the uneducated, unartful writer *(mother wits)*; and of the tradition of the irresponsible clown. In its stead is proposed the modulated and rhymeless line, and the wholly serious play. This play involves a high subject, *war*, and by implication and the enjoinment of decorum a *stately* style, a high and royal style. The effect will be largely one of language and of rhetoric, for there *you shall hear*, and you shall hear what is grand, or even grandiose, a *threatening the world*, expressed in *high astounding terms*.

Let us dwell on this phrase. A *term* is not any word, but a word belonging to a special vocabulary; so we speak of logical terms, and philosophical terms, and in the field of rhetoric there is, for example, that specialized literary diction which the Scots called "aureate terms." And Chaucer says in the *Canterbury Tales:*

> Youre termes, youre colours, and youre figures —
> Keep hem in stoor til so be that ye endite
> Heigh style, as whan that men to kinges write.
> *Clerk's Prologue,* 16-8

Tamburlaine will speak, then, in a choice and sifted language, the diction of *high* style, whose effect is here defined as that of wonder or astonishment, the *astounding*. This effect is supported by the kind of action involved, *scourging kingdoms with his conquering sword.*

The manifesto concludes with the proposition that the work of literature should merely present the object and leave the question of judgment to the spectator. This last, it seems to me, is Marlowe's one distinctive contribution to literary theory (I do not say that it is correct), and *Tamburlaine* is perhaps the only play of the period — perhaps the only play of Marlowe's — that clearly adheres to the doctrine. Yet it is only an extreme statement of a general trend in Elizabethan drama, the trend towards emancipating the story from the exemplum. However, it is the other ideas which are of concern here, and these ideas are the common critical property of the time. They enunciate the principle of high style, high characters, and high matters, to which Shakespeare gave allegiance, though a less thorough-going allegiance. The significance of this passage is that they are here expressed for the first time in Elizabethan drama, that they are expressed memorably, that the play to which these ideas are prologue is, if we leave aside Kyd and *The Spanish Tragedy*, the first notable application of the ideas, and, finally, that the play itself was a great success and had great influence on the course of Elizabethan drama.

The reader today is fairly unmoved by grand speeches, but the testimony of our fathers as to the overwhelming effect of the grand style is explicit and pretty unanimous. It should cause no surprise, then, to find that Shakespeare ascribes the quality of wonder to eloquence. He echoes *Tamburlaine* at the beginning of *I Henry the Sixth* (if the passage be indeed his); there the Dauphin, deeply impressed by Joan of Arc's long speech, exclaims seriously:

> Thou hast astonish'd me with thy high terms.
>
> 1. 2. 93

Again, in *Henry the Fifth* the Archbishop of Canterbury in delineating the ideal character of the King ascribes the same quality to the eloquence of theology and to the sweet style.

> Hear him but reason in divinity,
> And, all-admiring, with an inward wish
> You would desire the King were made a prelate. . .
> Turn him to any cause of policy,
> The Gordian knot of it he will unloose,
> Familiar as his garter; that, when he speaks,

> The air a charter'd libertine, is still,
> And the mute wonder lurketh in men's ears
> To steal his sweet and honey'd sentences. . .
>
> 1. 1. 38-40, 45-50

But the point is clear enough in *Hamlet* itself, and in connection with "tragical speeches." In the graveyard scene, after Laertes' outburst of rhetoric, Hamlet discloses himself and answers rant with rant:

> Nay, an thou'lt mouth,
> I'll rant as well as thou. . . .
>
> What is he whose grief
> Bears such an emphasis? whose phrase of sorrow
> Conjures the wand'ring stars, and makes them stand
> Like wonder-wounded hearers?
>
> 5. 1. 306-7, 277-80

The terms *emphasis* and *phrase* make quite clear that Hamlet refers to Laertes' style, which is at least intended to wound (that is, "to strike") the hearers with wonder.

Wonder in Shakespeare is the effect of tragic incident and tragic style, as well as of the marvellous turn in events. But this does not exhaust the complexity of the notion of wonder; one more strand at least remains to be unravelled. For the notion derives not only from the tradition of literary criticism, as the proper effect of marvellous events, and the tradition of rhetoric, as the proper effect of marvellous eloquence, but it derives also from the tradition of philosophy, in which wonder is the primary cause of learning.

Wonder, in this sense, is that which strikes our attention and provokes intensity of interest and intensity of curiosity. Hence it is obviously relevant to drama and fiction, for a story that does not interest us may as well not exist, as Mine Host will instruct us, who commented on the Monk's famous, but deadly, tragedies:

Sire Monk, namoore of this, so God you blesse! . . .
Nor certeinly, as that thise clerkes seyn,
Where as a man may have noon audience,
Noght helpeth it to tellen his sentence.

VII. 3978, 3990-2

It is especially relevant to the conclusions of Shakespearean plays, which are as persistently occupied with the explanation of "How these things came about" (*Hamlet*, 5. 2. 391) as are the conclusions of the modern detective story. For wonder, as the motive for acquiring knowledge, demands explanation and is satisfied by it. Now, to satisfy by explanation, though it may seem a misguided impulse to the modern reader who lives by the current maxim of "Never explain," was not unimportant to the Elizabethan: it is the chief concern of the dying Hamlet. He charges Horatio:

> report me and my cause aright
> To the unsatisfied. . . .
> O good Horatio, what a wounded name
> (Things standing thus unknown) shall live behind me!
> If thou didst ever hold me in thy heart,
> Absent thee from felicity awhile,
> And in this harsh world draw thy breath in pain,
> To tell my story.

5. 2. 350-1,355-60

For this reason, to satisfy the unsatisfied as to Hamlet's motives and actions, Horatio soon summarizes the events of the play, but not for this reason only. The unexplained gives scope to the irrational: hence

> let this same be presently perform'd
> Even while men's minds are wild, lest more mischance
> On plots and errors happen.

5. 2. 404-6

There is, then, in the resolution of wonder a kind of *catharsis*, a further effect of the effect of the catastrophe, and one appropriate to Shakespearean drama. To understand is to acquiesce. The movement of the drama is from this point of view an increasing intensity of interest which culminates in the striking events of the climax. These astonish the spectator so that he stands for the moment stone-still, but at the same time they demand explanation, and with the explanation his emotion subsides and order prevails, as on the stage at the close of the play order prevails in the state.

Certainly the philosophical notion of wonder enters into the explanation of the catastrophe. In the passage already cited from *Much Ado*, the Friar hastens to remark on the marvel of the catastrophe:

> All this amazement can I qualify,
> When, after that the holy rites are ended,
> I'll tell you largely of fair Hero's death.
>
> 5. 4. 67-9

First wonder, then explanation. So also in *As You Like It* Hymen, who enters to conclude the comedy, speaks thus:

> Peace ho! I bar confusion.
> 'Tis I must make conclusion
>   Of these most strange events . . .
> Whiles a wedlock hymn we sing,
> Feed yourselves with questioning,
> That reason wonder may diminish
> How thus we met, and these things finish.
>
> 5. 4. 131-3 and 143-6

And the general scheme is very well explained by Quince, as prologue to the "tragical mirth" that concludes *Midsummer Night's Dream*:

> Gentles, perchance you wonder at this show;
> But wonder on, till truth make all things plain.
>
> 5. 1. 128-9

To sum up: the primary effect of tragedy is sorrow or woe, of which pity is a species. The tragic atmosphere and the incidents leading to the catastrophe are fearful. This is the Donatan tradition in which the tragic fact is violent, unexpected death, and corresponds to the medieval tradition of psychology in which the anticipation of death is fearful and its accomplishment woful. But since the catastrophe is unexpected, it will startle the audience, and so the emotion of fear which has accompanied the course of tragic incident will become attached in special measure to the catastrophe. But this will be that fear which results from external events: wonder, astonishment, or shocked surprise. Hence woe and wonder are the effects of the tragic spectacle. Horatio's phrase, then, as is Sidney's, is only a distillation of the tradition, and *woe* is even a more proper term than pity, *wonder* than fear.

In the preceding section, I have cited texts in which Shakespeare explicitly names wonder as an effect of tragic incident, of tragic style, and as the principal effect of the catastrophe of those non-tragical plays which involve marvellous events, being the natural correlative of marvels and the motive for understanding them. But is wonder named in any other work of Shakespeare as an effect of the tragic catastrophe, or does it appear only in the one passage from *Hamlet?* Again, is it customary to name explicitly the intended effect at the end of other Elizabethan plays?

It will be expected that woe or pity will be the most commonly named, and in fact there are more texts than anyone wishes to look through. To cite one example, the anonymous *Tragedy of Locrine* is drenched with mournful complaints. These occur after each of the successive tragic catastrophes which constitute the play (1. 1. 227 ff.; 3. 1. 1 ff.; and especially 43 ff.; 3. 6. 1 ff.; 5. 1. 1 ff. and especially 16 ff.), but most notably at the end. Here in Estrild's lament over the death of Locrine, the concept of lamentation and pity is explicitly associated with the concept of tragedy as involving both the fall and death of the great, and the lesson of the instability of this world — for here as in glass we plainly see that all our life is but as a tragedy, a confused chaos of mishaps:

> Break, heart, with sobs and generous suspires!
> Stream forth, you tears, from forth my watery eyes!
> Help me to mourn for warlike Locrine's death!
> Pour down your tears, you watery regions,
> For mighty Locrine is bereft of life!
> O fickle Fortune! O unstable world!
> What else are all things that this globe contains
> But a confused chaos of mishaps?
> Wherein as in a glass we plainly see
> That all our life is but as a tragedy,
> Since mighty kings are subject to mishap . . .
>   5. 4. 111-21[25]

But the effect of wonder is common enough. In Greene's *Orlando Furioso* the Emperor of Africa, who is the representative of the state, replies after hearing an account of the action from Orlando:

> I stand amazed, deep overdrenched with joy,
> To hear and see this unexpected end:
> So will I rest content.
>   5. 2. 1425-7[26]

This is the kind of wonder we have already met at the end of the *Winter's Tale*. Of like kind is the effect of the discovery in Marston's *Malcontent* that Malevole is Altofont, the former and legitimate Duke of Genoa:

> MALEVOLE. Banish amazement; come, we four must stand
> Full shock of fortune. Be not so wonder stricken. . . .
> PIETRO. . . . Give leave to recollect
> My thoughts dispersed in wild astonishment.
>   4. 5

This is the principal catastrophe of the play, though there follows in the fifth act, amid masquing and comedy, a second reversal — the fall of Mendoza. Of a similar nature is the discovery of Andrugio at the end of Marston's *Antonio and Mellida*:

> We are amazed, our royal spirits numbed
> In stiff astonished wonder at thy prowess . . .

And, a little later, when Antonio rises from the coffin:

> Stand not amazed, great states! . . .
> Most wished spectators of my tragedy. . . .

There is a different, but not too dissimilar, kind in the 1610 *Mucedorus*, the version played before King James. Here Comedy and Envy in the Epilogue suddenly kneel before the majesty of James:

> ENVY. My power has lost her might; Envy's date's expired.
> Yon splendent majesty hath felled my sting,
> And I amazed am. *Fall down and quake.*
>
> 65-7[28]

But for wonder as the immediate effect of the catastrophe of a tragic, rather than of a comic or heroic, catastrophe, Shakespeare himself gives precedent. The catastrophe of Shakespeare's poem the *Rape of Lucrece* is Lucrece's suicide — at which:

> Stone-still, astonish'd with this deadly deed,
> Stood Collatine and all his lordly crew. . .
>
> 1730-1

This is the wonder that is a species of fear; but, as the shock subsides, woe and pity rise:

> About the mourning and congealed face
> Of that black blood a wat'ry rigoll goes,
> Which seems to weep upon the tainted place;
> And ever since, as pitying Lucrece' woes,
> Corrupted blood some watery token shows, . . .
>
> 1744-48

The poem ends finally with Brutus' speech, which again provokes wonder:

> This said, he struck his hand upon his breast
> And kiss'd the fatal knife to end his vow;
> And to his protestation urg'd the rest,
> Who, wond'ring at him, did his words allow.
>
> 1842-5

Quite parallel to this is the conclusion of Jonson's *Sejanus*.
Here signs and prodigies precede the fall of Sejanus:

> But now a fiery meteor in the form
> Of a great ball was seen to roll along
> The troubled air, where yet it hangs unperfect,
> The amazing wonder of the multitude!
>
> 5. 4. 48-51

The fall itself provokes wonder:

> MACRO. Wherefore, fathers,
> Sit you amazed and silent . . .
>
> 5. 10. 246-7

But the final effect is a curious kind of terror, emotionally
rather subtle, for, though terror is not directly named, no one
can miss it: the more our pity is solicited in the subsequent
speeches for the attendant circumstances of Sejanus' fall, the
more our terror rises. The pity which these accounts summon
is really a kind of aghast terror at the mob and at the political
corruption which still persists and is not resolved with Sejanus'
fall. The pity we feel is certainly not pity for Sejanus himself,
who had disclaimed any such softness:

> When I do fear again, let me be struck
> With forked fire, and unpitied die . . .
>
> 5. 6. 75-6

to whom it had been denied by Macro:

> And no man take compassion of thy state . . .
>
> 5. 10. 242

and whose fall is described thus by Lepidus:

> And this man fall! Fall? Ay, without a look
> That durst appear his friend, or lend so much
> Of vain relief to his changed state as pity!
>
> 5. 10. 283-5

Finally Arruntius at the very end of the play sums it all up:

> Forbear, you things
> That stand upon the pinnacles of state
> To boast your slippery height: when you do fall
> You pash yourselves to pieces, ne'er to rise;
> And he who lends you pity is not wise.
>
> 5. 10. 458-62[29]

The immediate effect of the fall is wonder, but its final effect is a terror begotten by the detailing of the occasions for pity. But the pity is simply for the human state and the innocent bystanders; there can be no real pity for the fall of a thorough villain. And here is disclosed how fear or terror enters properly into the catastrophe of an Elizabethan play. We feel pity for the death of the good and for death itself, but the violent end of the wicked begets fear. Thus Shakespeare's Queen Margaret anticipates the fall of Richard III:

> But at hand, at hand
> Ensues his piteous and unpitied end.
>
> 4. 4. 73-4

and Richmond later comes from the field of battle:

> God and your arms be prais'd, victorious friends!
> The day is ours; the bloody dog is dead.
>
> 5. 5. 1-2

Contrast this with Bolingbroke's comment on Richard II, who was weak but not villainous:

> Lords, I protest my soul is full of woe
> That blood should sprinkle me to make me grow.

101

> Come, mourn with me for what I do lament. . .
>> 5. 6. 45-7

In like fashion the death of Macbeth is not mourned — he is spoken of as "this dead butcher and his fiendlike queen" (5. 8. 69) — though that of Siward's son is:

> Your cause of sorrow
> Must not be measur'd by his worth, for then
> It hath no end.
>> 5. 8. 44-6

    Sorrow and pity are reserved for the deaths of the good, or for the human fact itself — even Richard III's end will be piteous, though unpitied. Hence, at the end of *Lear*, Albany, the representative of the state, says after the deaths of Lear and Cordelia:

> Bear them from hence. Our present business
> Is general woe.
>> 5. 3. 318-19

But on the earlier reported deaths of Goneril and Regan, one of whom was his wife, he only says:

> This judgement of the heavens, that makes us tremble,
> Touches us not with pity.
>> 5. 3. 231-2

Fear, then, is the effect of the violent death of the wicked as distinguished from that of the good, whose fall evokes sorrow and pity.

    The striking effect of pity and sorrow is explicitly named at the end of two later Shakespearean tragedies. Octavian, the representative of the state, sums up *Antony and Cleopatra*:

> High events as these
> Strike those that make them; and their story is
> No less in pity than his glory which
> Brought them to be lamented.
>> 5. 2. 363-6

The verb *strike* here denotes the effect of wonder — at least, this is its ordinary meaning. Aufidius utters similar sentiments at the end of *Coriolanus:*

> My rage is gone,
> And I am struck with sorrow. Take him up.

Again, to be struck is the effect of wonder. Consequently, these three plays at least — *Hamlet, Anthony and Cleopatra, Coriolanus* — together with the *Rape of Lucrece,* are intended explicitly to evoke the emotional effect of woe and wonder.

From the later tradition I will quote only the following close parallel: The Cardinal in Middleton's *Women Beware Women* characterizes the catastrophe thus:

> The greatest sorrow and astonishment
> That ever struck the general peace of Florence
> Dwells in this hour.
>
> 5. 1. 240-2[30]

V

Reason Panders Will

The emotional effect of the catastrophe, of course, is not equivalent to the experience of the work. It is a final element in that experience, enters into it, and in part determines it. But there is more to the experience of art than the emotional effect even of the whole, and certainly more than the effect of the conclusion. There is, among other things, the experience of the language of the work. There is, especially in the Renaissance, the intellectual experience of persistent sententious thought. And there is in the typical play the central intellectual experience of plotting, counter-plotting, and mistakes: the events of *Hamlet* are characterized by Horatio at the end of the play as "mischance" that "on plots and errors happen" (5. 2. 405-6). This is an experience of the same sort as that of a game of chess, and is like chess intense in its kind, for though it is intellectual it is not without emotion: otherwise it would not be experience. Nevertheless, the other aspects of a work are related to the effect of the conclusion, and not only as elements in the larger experience of the whole. They are related in this way: though the effect itself is largely a result of the bare fact, of what happens, it is not sufficient merely to attain an effect; the effect must be justified. We must acquiesce in the conclusion.

We acquiesce out of a feeling of inevitability: what will be will be. But what is the source of this feeling? A conclusion is inevitable *within the closed system of a work of art* when it satisfies a pattern or principle of order acceptable to the audience. Such patterns are of different kinds, some larger, some smaller. They may be external, as, for example, the full circuit of Fortune's wheel, the fulfilment of the retributive justice of

God, or the progression from order to disorder, concluding sadly in deaths. The pattern may exhibit the causal sequence of realistic fiction, which consists in an exemplification of a syllogistic conclusion (more precisely, an enthymeme) made persuasive. For a causal sequence shows a probable course of action, and by probability we mean a conformity to some accepted commonplace about how men of a certain type will behave under certain conditions. This is persuasive when sharply and compellingly presented so that we do not explicitly recognize the syllogistic nature of the conclusion. We merely believe it, speak of it as if it were really determined, and hence inevitable. We say the conclusion was logical.

The pattern may, however, be internal and involve artistic foreshadowing and completion, suggestion and fulfilment. Artistic devices of this nature are usually referred to and grounded on the personality of the characters, and so exhibit that adjustment of feeling which comprises the ethics of sensibility. Or, and this is quite different, the pattern may be internal and involve the structure of character. In this case it will exhibit responsibility and moral choice, and will exemplify the ethics of character. Of this sort is the pattern or principle of order which is the subject of this essay. It is only one among many, but it will serve to illustrate the kinds of principles I have in mind and the relationship of these to the emotional effect of the conclusion.

The basic text for this principle of order in Renaissance tragedy is the definition of tragedy in Averroës' paraphrase of Aristotle's *Poetics,* which was current throughout the later Middle Ages and was probably more widely reprinted in the Renaissance than the work of any other commentator. The definition reads:

> Tragedy is the imitative representation of a notable action, brought to completion by a voluntary decision, and having in it a certain force of generalization with respect to matters of

105

some import, as distinguished from a particular proposition about some individual fact. By means of this imitative representation there is induced in the minds of the audience a rightness of feeling which springs from the pity and terror which the representation begets in them.[1]

The final effect of tragedy according to this definition is ethical: it results in an ordering of the irrational by means of a presentation which evokes specific emotional effects. The internal spring of the plot is a willed act, or moral choice. The final cause is right feeling, which is obviously the correlative of the ethical principle of right reason. This rightness of feeling comes through the tragic emotions, but apparently the effective cause of ordered feeling is the force of generalization in the plot. The universal here is an immanent power, not explicit or allegorical, and not singular or particular.[2]

Some of the greater tragedies of Shakespeare correspond well enough to this definition, which supplements the Donatan tradition with, among other principles, the principle of action involving moral choice. But choice in tragedy is usually a choice of evil, and hence the question in Renaissance terms is one of sin. How does a man sin? There are two main views in the Renaissance, the intellectualist view of the Aristotelian and Thomistic tradition, and the voluntarist view whose tradition is more complex. In the former the act of sin is primarily intellectual so that the process involves erroneous reasoning: action follows on reasoned deliberation as the conclusion of a syllogism follows on its premises. The will is considered to be subservient to reason and to embrace almost necessarily what reason proposes. Erroneous choice, then, from this position will be ascribed primarily to sophistry. Practical reason in the possession of the immutable principles of right action fails in the particular application, and so sins. In Duns Scotus' phrase, "We sin by paralogism." For the will never moves except "under the show of goodness," as Thomas says,[3] or, as Iago puts it in *Othello:*

> Divinity of hell!
> When devils will the blackest sins put on,
> They do suggest at first with heavenly shows,
> As I do now.
>
> 2. 3. 356-9

We may account for sin, then, by saying that it is the result of a logical confusion, a failure to discriminate between *a* good and *the* good. Thus in the case of Macbeth it will be granted that the kingship is *a* good, but it was not for Macbeth *the* good. The irrational part of the soul, the passions and perturbations, will affect man, so long as he remains man and is in the possession of his faculties, only to the extent that his reason may be sophisticated so that he accepts invalid for valid argument. For, "if the passions of the mind be strong," Hooker relates, "they easily sophisticate the understanding; they make it apt to believe upon very slender warrant, and to imagine infallible truth where scarcely any probable show appeareth" (*EP*, 5. Dedication). In brief, reason is not dethroned or suspended, but is perverted, commits an error in logic, and is actively enlisted on the side of false desire. The process is one of reasonable choice though the reasonableness be unreasonable. It is briefly summed up in a phrase in *Hamlet*: "reason panders will."

The phrase occurs in the closet scene. It is in its context the last and most violent in a series of illustrations of the perversion of the natural order of things. Hamlet says to his mother:

> Rebellious hell,
> If thou canst mutine in a matron's bones,
> To flaming youth let virtue be as wax
> And melt in her own fire. Proclaim no shame
> When the compulsive ardour gives the charge,
> Since frost itself as actively does burn,
> And reason panders will.
>
> 3. 4. 82-8

Rhetorically, this is a very curious passage. It is a series of adynata, of impossibilities. As such, it employs the tritest device of classical and Renaissance rhetoric. We are accustomed to sigh when we meet it. But these are adynata in an ethical context; they are impossibilities only to right reason and uncorrupted nature. To be sure, frost from the point of view of Renaissance science cannot burn as if it were active. But every observer of Renaissance and fallen man knew that lust not only could but regularly did break out, even in those in whom by age and station it was especially indecorous. And every Christian knew that man was inherently sinful, and that the state of sin was that in which reason pandered will. Yet he knew that these perversions of the due order were not right, and he would feel the moral horror that Hamlet, and Shakespeare, expresses by this rhetorical device: the horror that these impossibilities, repugnant to Reason and true Nature, should be not merely possible but actual and in our sense almost natural.

The phrase, then, expresses nothing new in the history of thought. The idea is at least as old as Aristotle; it is, in fact, a compendious statement of the Aristotelian analysis of the act of erroneous moral choice which had been taken up, developed, and rendered almost conventional by a long line of medieval and Renaissance philosophers. In this tradition when reason panders will the due and proper subordination of the irrational to the rational is overturned, and overturned the more grievously in that reason is not merely suspended or dethroned but is actively enlisted in the service of desire. The man who is swept away by emotion acts unreasonably and wrongly but not perversely; the man whose reason is bent to further his unreasonable desires is in that measure diabolical.

As idea, then, it was available and in a sense trite. It had already been employed by Shakespeare, most clearly in one passage which may be regarded as the direct ancestor of this. The passage is in the reply of Adonis to the arguments of

108

Venus in *Venus and Adonis,* for it was the quaint device of the Elizabethans to believe in discourse of reason, and they would seem, if we may accept the testimony of their literature, even to have attempted seduction by the method of disputation, and by the same method to have repelled it. Such is the case with Comus and the Lady in Milton's poem. And as the Lady in *Comus* extricates herself from the designs of the villain by opposing true reason to false reasoning, true love to earthly lust:

> I had not thought to have unlockt my lips
> In this unhallowed air but that this juggler
> Would think to charm my judgement as mine eyes,
> Obtruding false rules pranked in reason's garb.
>
> 756-9

so Adonis answers Venus' arguments and defines in context the nature of sin:

> What have you urg'd that I cannot reprove?
> The path is smooth that leadeth on to danger.
> I hate not love, but your device in love,
> That lends embracements unto every stranger.
> You do it for increase. O strange excuse,
> When reason is the bawd to lust's abuse!
>
> 787-92

Here the idea is more fully and more analytically presented than in the phrase in *Hamlet,* though less fully and less analytically than in Thomas or Aristotle. To achieve the later phrase there remained only to subject this passage to the Shakespearean transmutation: to turn idea into intuition, to condense it to three words, and by the metaphorical *panders,* a violent and sensuous word, to exhibit reason and will as sinful and shabby figures in a disreputable world.

But though this was the orthodox view, resting on the long Aristotelian tradition, it was not the only view at that time. Erroneous action was often presented in Elizabethan drama as the result of the dethroning of reason. This latter possibility is allowed for in the Scholastic scheme, for it is an

109

obvious fact of experience, but it is minimized. Thomas says, for example, that in cases of sudden and violent emotion, when reason cannot come to the opposition, mortal sin is not involved. But this is only a limiting case. For if the passion, say of love or anger, were in its origin voluntary the consequences would involve sin even though the passion took away the use of reason entirely. The critical point of decision is simply moved further back. Only if the cause were not voluntary but natural, as for example some bodily sickness, would the consequences be excused of sin (*ST*, 1-2. 77. 7).

Nevertheless, interest in the limiting case grew in the Renaissance. The full history of this development is somewhat obscure but the principal lines are clear. In the first place, there was the development of a mechanistic psychology, the Galenic psychology of humors, with its emphasis on the involuntariness of strong passion; the most famous text in English is Burton's *Anatomy of Melancholy*. In the second place, there was the development of a voluntaristic metaphysics in the Franciscan school associated with the name of Duns Scotus, and the subsequent extension of this point of view to ethics. The issue of this movement was the predestinarianism of the Reformation with its emphasis on the helplessness of man, and particularly of his reason, and the corollary interest in Stoic Fate, which was supported by the prestige of Seneca's tragedies. Here, especially in the *Phaedra,* as also in Ovid's Medea, were classic exemplars of tragic characters swept away by an overmastering passion: "I see the better course, and approve of it; I follow the worse."[4] It is curious that this view of human action which ascribes to the will, the faculty of inner motion in man, the ultimate control of his destiny should in practice have issued often in an extreme determinism. Perhaps this is a sign of the thoroughgoing rationalism of the period; the more the will was considered to be irresponsible to the dictates of reason and free to act arbitrarily, the more some principle of compulsion must be invoked to account for the irresponsible arbitrariness of the will.

But whatever the reasons, there are at least four sorts of compulsion to be found in Elizabethan drama. There is, first, the compulsion which is accounted for by a mechanistic physiology and psychology, a type that has been studied a good deal in recent years, notably by Mr. Hardin Craig. He points out, for example, that the sudden and apparently unmotivated jealousy of Leontes in the *Winter's Tale* is explainable in such terms:[5]

> Too hot, too hot!
> To mingle friendship far, is mingling bloods.
> I have tremor cordis on me; my heart dances,
> But not for joy; not joy.
>
> 1. 2. 108-10

I have tremor cordis on me. But Leontes' jealousy is conceived also as voluntaristic, as involving the primacy of feeling. This is explicit in the key line of the speech in which Leontes embraces his unjustified jealousy:

> Can thy dam—may't be?
> Affection! thy intention stabs the centre.
>
> 1. 2. 137-8

Affection denotes the passions, emotions, and feelings which are associated with the will in the moving faculty of the soul, as distinguished from the rational faculty to which the will is attached as the rational appetite. *Intention* denotes the directed movement of a faculty of the soul toward realizing a possibility. It is that which is required to raise the potentiality of knowledge to act, and it is also the movement by which the rational will tends toward and embraces the end of action proposed by reason.[6] The passage means, then, that affection directing its own movement, penetrates to the knowledge of the fact which gives the grounds for being jealous, and at the same time embraces the decision to be jealous. Hence we may translate Leontes' speech into modern terms: "Feeling rather than reason hits the mark and furnishes the decision." This is explicit voluntarism.

The third type of compulsion is that exercised by the Stoic Fate, and operating often through the influence of the stars. The fourth is the theological compulsion of grace and predestination. The two are conjoined and offered as alternative explanations of the tragic action in Heywood's *A Woman Killed with Kindness*. The tragic villain speaks:

> I am a villian if I apprehend
> But such a thought! Then, to attempt the deed,
> Slave, thou art damn'd without redemption.—
> I'll drive away this passion with a song.
> A song! Ha, ha! A song! As if, fond man,
> Thy eyes could swim in laughter, when thy soul
> Lies drench'd and drowned in red tears of blood!
> I'll pray, and see if God within my heart
> Plant better thoughts. Why, prayers are meditations,
> And when I meditate (oh, God forgive me!)
> It is on her divine perfections.
> I will forget her; I will arm myself
> Not t'entertain a thought of love to her;
> And, when I come by chance into her presence,
> I'll hale these balls until my eye-strings crack,
> From being pull'd and drawn to look that way.
>
> > *Enter, over the Stage, Frankford, his Wife,*
> > *and Nick*
>
> O God, O God! With what a violence
> I'm hurried to mine own destruction!
>
> > > 2. 3. 1-18

And again:

> I will not; zounds! I will not. I may choose,
> And I will choose. Shall I be so misled,
> Or shall I purchase to my father's crest
> The motto of a villain? If I say
> I will not do it, what thing can enforce me?
> What can compel me? What sad destiny

112

Hath such command upon my yielding thoughts?
I will not;—ha! Some fury pricks me on;
The swift fates drag me at their chariot wheel,
And hurry me to mischief.

2. 3. 96-105

The tragic action follows. And since the first citation above is a soliloquy and the second an aside, they may be taken as representing the view of tragic motivation which the author himself proffers. This is one of sheer fatalism. The character attempts to distract his thoughts, as Thomas for example suggests he should (*ST*, 1-2. 77. 2: "Whether reason can be overcome by passion against its knowledge"), but the divine sensuality of love overpowers him. He attempts to exercise rational choice, but fury and Fate hurry him to mischief, and with him the other characters. He sees the better course and approves it, but follows the worse. Yet an alternative explanation, which could be regarded as the same explanation under another aspect, is given at the end of the play. Here the leading character, a good man, sums up the whole:

God, that hath laid this cross upon our heads,
Might (had He pleas'd) have made our cause of meeting
On a more fair and more contented ground;
But He that made us made us to this woe.[7]

For what seems to man to be a result of Fate or fury is but the concealed operation of the Providence of God.

The contrast between the intellectual and voluntarist positions can be made clear by comparing Sextus Tarquin's soliloquy before committing the rape in Heywood's play *The Rape of Lucrece* with the similar soliloquy in Shakespeare's poem of the same title. In the former Tarquin enters Lucrece's bedchamber carrying a drawn sword and a lighted taper. He speaks:

I am bound
Upon a black adventure, on a deed
That must wound virtue and make beauty bleed.

113

Pause, Sextus, and, before thou runnst thyself
Into this violent danger, weigh thy sin. . .
       Back! yet thy fame
Is free from hazard and thy style from shame.
O Fate! thou hast usurped such power o'er man
That where thou pleadst thy will no mortal can. . .
       Forward still!
To make thy lust live, all thy virtues kill.

4. 3[8]

Certainly reasonable deliberation in the sense of rational awareness is involved here as it was in the previous citation from *A
Woman Killed with Kindness*. But it does not enter into the
decision. The character in the grip of strong emotion must act
contrary to the dictates of reason: Fate sweeps him on. He
makes no attempt to justify his sin; the end is not presented
under the show of goodness.

But in Shakespeare's poem the poet himself explains the
course of Tarquin's soliloquy:

Thus, graceless, holds he disputation
'Tween frozen conscience and hot burning will,
And with good thoughts makes dispensation,
Urging the worser sense for vantage still;
Which in a moment doth confound and kill
    All pure effects, and doth so far proceed
    That what is vile shows like a virtuous deed.

246-52

God for his own inscrutable reasons does not assist Tarquin on
this occasion with his grace *(Thus, graceless)*. Hence Tarquin
must reach this moral decision on a human and ethical plane.
And how is the process described? It is described in medieval
terms as the holding of a disputation. In this disputation
Tarquin urges the worser sense for vantage still; reason is
actively enlisted in the service of desire. When the process
reaches the point of decision it doth in a moment confound all

114

pure effects, for Tarquin by the decision has sinned mortally. Consequently, the undoing—not of his character, really, in the modern sense, but of his moral principle—doth so far proceed that what is vile shows like a virtuous deed. He sins by paralogism under the show of goodness.

II

The act of decision in the intellectualist tradition has as a further characteristic mark that it is divided into two steps: the choice of the end *(intentio)* and the choice of means *(electio)*. The steps are distinct, though the second is dependent on the first (*ST*, 1-2. 8. 3). I shall now analyze two scenes in Shakespearean tragedy, one in *Othello* and one in *Macbeth,* each of which portrays an act of moral choice that leads to the catastrophe; and I shall conclude with a discussion of the whole scope of *Hamlet.*

The scene in *Othello* concerns the choice of the end, for there is here no serious question of means. Othello has it in his power to kill Desdemona at any time, and presuming his grounds are correct the killing is justified. "Cassio did top her," he says to Emilia:

> Oh, I were damn'd beneath all depth in hell
> But that I did proceed upon just grounds
> To this extremity.
>
> 5. 2. 136-9

As for the death of Cassio, Iago promises to take care of that. The only question, then, is the question of fact; for it is assumed in the play, and made more plausible by locating the action in Venice and Cyprus, that if Desdemona has been unfaithful she must die.

The action of the play, so far as it concerns the moral act, is roughly this: Iago plants in Othello's mind the idea that his wife may be unfaithful, and he does it so skilfully that he is not himself open to attack. The mere idea is sufficient to upset most men:

> Dangerous conceits are in their nature poisons
> Which at the first are scarce found to distaste,
> But with a little act upon the blood
> Burn like the mines of sulphur.
>
> 3. 3. 326-9

But Iago does more than plant the idea; he insinuates a number of fairly vivid and violent images; he raises an efficient head of passion. More than this, he brings to bear on the question a number of commonplaces which make the fact more credible: women are weak; most husbands are cuckolds. He shows that in this special situation infidelity is even more likely, for as Desdemona has deceived her father so she may deceive him. Besides, there is the fact of their disproportion in race, in age, and in social position. Any man would be almost convinced of his wife's infidelity after such insinuation.

But its effect on Othello is only to get him into a passion in which he may do anything. He may even, as he threatens, kill Iago. At this point Iago intervenes with an appeal to reason:

> Are you a man? have you a soul? or sense?[9]
>
> 3. 3. 374

That is, "Are you a man or beast? Have you a rational soul, since reason is the distinguishing characteristic of man? or merely sense, the sensitive soul, the distinguishing characteristic of animals?" He appeals to reason because he does not want to put Othello merely in a passion; there can be no directed action without a reasoned conclusion. And Othello answers this appeal by stating the disjunctive syllogism upon which the play turns:

> I think my wife be honest, and think she is not;
> I think that thou art just, and think thou art not.
> I'll have some proof.
>
> 3. 3. 384-6

But he has prefaced this with the statement, "Nay, stay. Thou shouldst be honest." And it has been reiterated throughout the play, not without purpose, that Iago is honest. So when the disjunction is presented almost in technical form: Either Iago is honest or Desdemona is honest, the conclusion that: Iago is honest, therefore Desdemona is not, is almost guaranteed by the assumption that Iago is. Hence Othello goes on:

> Her name, that was as fresh
> As Dian's visage, is now begrim'd and black
> As mine own face.

Nevertheless, Othello's feeling is so strong he does not yet assent; he demands some proof. If he cannot see his wife strumpeted before his eyes, let him at least have some circumstantial sign. However, as Iago has confided to the audience (3. 3. 321-4), Othello, in the distraught state of mind in which he is prepared to assent to the syllogism proposed, will accept as proof the flimsiest trifle of a sign, a mere handkerchief which he saw really but a moment ago. When to this is added Iago's account of Cassio's remarks in his sleep, which is accepted substantially as testimony to a confession on Cassio's part, the cause is finished. Othello consents. "Patience, I say," Iago interposes, "your mind perhaps may change." "Never, Iago" (3. 3. 452-3). The choice is made and solemnly ratified by oath. The following scene (3. 4 together with 4. 1 and 2) supports the decision but is subsequent to it. The play moves on to the catastrophe.

No one cares to see such things happen. Nevertheless, we can acquiesce since we can see "How these things came about." A man "not easily jealous" is operated on by a skilful insinuator and becomes so "perplex'd in the extreme" that his passions easily sophisticate his understanding: "they make it apt to believe upon very slender warrant, and to imagine infallible truth where scarcely any probable show appeareth." Othello is perplexed both intellectually and emotionally, but primarily

117

intellectually. For, as Francis Bacon relates in the *Advancement of Learning*, there is a seducement that works by the subtlety of the illaqueation and another by the strength of the impression. The latter overmasters the reason by power of sense and imagination; the former works by perplexing the reason.[10] The process is described more fully in a sermon by Bishop Andrewes with reference to the fall of Eve:

> For this is not the least policy of the Devil, not to set upon her bluntly, but like a serpent slily and slowly to creep in her little by little, until he has espied some vantage. Therefore his order is: to bring her from questioning in talk to a doubt in opinion, and from that to an error in judgement, and so at last to a corrupt action in practice. And to corrupt her mind within, first he useth this order, to tickle her ears with curiosity, and by that to cause her to have a giddiness and swimming in the brain by fantastical imaginations and surmises; and then to make her secure and careless of the truth, and so at last maketh her somewhat inclinable to error and falsehood.[11]

But Othello's transition to jealousy and sin has not seemed plausible to every reader. It is not true to life, we are told, and the theatrical convention of the calumniator credited has been invented to solve the difficulty.[12] But the crediting of calumny is no mere convention of the theatre; it is a fact of daily life The truth is, the modern critic is concerned to defend the niceness of life, to maintain that successful hypocrisy is unlikely, that no one omits speaking up when he should, that no decent husband suspects his precious wife, and that if he does they just talk it over like civilized people. Anyway, no woman of character will sleep with a man's best friend.

Such critics make the optimistic assumption that men are not likely to go wrong unless there is sufficient cause. But this is modern, and not too well founded in fact. The general assumption of the Renaissance was that men were not likely to go right unless there was a supernatural cause. "Such is the propensity of all creatures unto evil," Bishop Jewel says,

118

"and the readiness of all men to suspect, that the things which neither have been done, nor once meant to be done, yet may be easily both heard and credited for true."[13] The modern critic feels that women do not tend to be unfaithful; the Renaissance man, who was still smarting under Eve's transgression, felt that women were pretty likely to be unfaithful if they only had a chance. He would take Othello's remarks on cuckoldry as hardly exaggerated:

> 'Tis destiny unshunnable, like death.
> Even then this forked plague is fated to us
> When we do quicken.
>
> 3. 3. 275-7

Furthermore, the appeal of Desdemona's innocency is much greater for the reader than it was for Othello; he knows she is innocent, which is precisely what Othello does not know.

Anyone who is willing to believe in evil, and personally I do not find this difficult to do, will not find Othello's jealousy implausible. He may be worried, however, that it all seems to happen in so short a time, and he may wonder just how it is that Othello seems to be convinced that his wife is unfaithful —not how Iago persuades him, for that is clear enough, but by what process he comes to accept the proposition himself. I have held that the process is the traditional one of moral choice and intellectualist in character. For all his passion Othello is not swept away; he is presented with a disjunctive syllogism, draws what seems to him a proper conclusion, confirms the conclusion with a sign, and proceeds upon what he thinks are just grounds to this extremity. The process of choice, itself, takes place in a point of time and is properly represented as occurring within a single scene.

The restriction of the process of choice to a point of time and a single scene contributes to the feeling of implausibility. Our natural tendency, as can be seen in the novel, is to consider the process of choice as distributed through a number of scenes

119

and as in large measure unconscious. We tend to find the condensed incredible and the diffused plausible. We regard decision as so implicated in the circumstances that condition it that neither can profitably be distinguished from the other. We can believe anything if only it be an indistinct compound of environment and heredity, and if we can be persuaded that it has evolved. For what is perhaps the greatest single difference between our habits of thought and those of the Middle Ages and Renaissance is located in the problem of continuity. We believe in the continuous. We believe that contraries shade off into each other. We believe a character is real when he is neither good nor bad but a middling gray. We disbelieve in, though we have not yet disproved, the law of the excluded middle. But the Renaissance believed firmly in Aristotelian logic: for them, B was either A or Not-A.

They also believed firmly in sin and repentance, each of which takes place in a point of time. Sin and grace were precise contraries that could not shade off into each other. Hence their view of the moral life was radically different from ours; it was essentially theological. Man's destiny hung on each decisive act, a life of grace could be cancelled by one mortal sin, and conversely the departing soul of an old and confirmed sinner could, though it was not likely, at the furthest margin of life repent of his sins and so pass joyously into the company of the elect. Such a view was held by both the great parties in the theological wars of the sixteenth century; it was proclaimed openly by those who emphasized man's free choice, but it was also maintained, if paradoxically maintained, by many of the fiercest proponents of predestination. For though a man be predestined to Hell, still he must wilfully embrace that act by which he is eternally condemned, for the responsibility must be his and not the predestinating God's. So likewise, if he be predestined to Heaven, though he make an ungodly life his profession, still at the predestined moment he shall have grace to repent and his will must embrace that repentance. It is clear, then, that the restriction of the process of choice in Elizabethan drama to a single scene is not the result merely of foreshortening and condensation for dramatic purposes, but is a result of the Elizabethan view of the moral life. At the same time, of course, it is more dramatic.

The process of the decisive choice of evil can be seen more clearly, and this time with respect to the choice of means, in one scene in *Macbeth*.[14] It is the seventh of the first act. Macbeth enters and announces in a soliloquy that he has already fallen from the state of grace, that he has preferred the show of goodness in things temporal to the solid goodness of things eternal:

> If it were done when 'tis done, then 'twere well
> It were done quickly. If th' assassination
> Could trammel up the consequence, and catch,
> With his surcease, success; that but this blow
> Might be the be-all and the end-all here,
> But here, upon this bank and shoal of time,
> We'ld jump the life to come.
>
> 1. 7. 1-7

His will has already moved to embrace the end, the kingship, but he is disturbed. He does not see how to accomplish it; he does not see how he can get away with the murder of Duncan:

> But in these cases
> We still have judgement here, that we but teach
> Bloody instructions, which, being taught, return
> To plague th' inventor.
>
> 1. 7. 7-10

Thus there is a consequent weakening of the will:

> I have no spur
> To prick the sides of my intent, but only
> Vaulting ambition, which o'erleaps itself
> And falls on th' other side.
>
> 1. 7. 25-8

Enter Lady Macbeth.

To understand what follows it will be well to recapitulate the requirements for a moral act. Reason must propose an end as good, and when the end is proposed the will moves naturally to embrace it. This has already happened in Macbeth, but it is not sufficient to constitute moral choice. The practical reason must discover means by which to accomplish the end *(consilium)*, and not until the means are available is the choice finally made. There must follow sufficient emotion *(consensus)* so that the choice is actually put into operation *(usus)*. This emotion precedes, accompanies, and follows the act of choice. It is the steam pressure that makes the engine move; there must be a certain excitement in the will to account for the step to choice and from choice to action. It is the office of rhetoric to supply this excitement; its function is to persuade. So Bacon defines it in a passage that has often been quoted but usually not properly understood: "The duty and office of rhetoric is to apply reason to imagination for the better moving of the will."[15] By *apply* here is meant "to put into practical contact with," so that if one were to use these words in a modern context he would rather say that imagination is applied to reason.

The traditional analysis, popularized and lacking the complication of multiplied distinctions, is expounded by the character of Tragedy himself in a play which was presented by Shakespeare's company (ca. 1598) a few years before *Hamlet*. *A Warning to Fair Women* begins with an argument between Tragedy, Comedy, and History. Later in the play, at the moment of moral choice, Tragedy steps forward and explains the process:

> Prevailing sin having by three degrees
> Made his ascension to forbidden deeds,
> At first, alluring their unwary minds
> To like what she proposed, then practising
> To draw them to consent; and, last of all,
> Ministering fit means and opportunity

To execute what she approved good;
Now she unveils their sight, and lets them see
The horror of their foul immanity.

2. 865-74[16]

But to return to *Macbeth*. He has embraced the end, and
now falters in resolution because he does not see how the end
can be accomplished. There is required now fit means and
opportunity to execute what he approved good, together with
a concurrent sustaining and heightening of resolution, the
maintaining of an efficient head of passion. To fulfill this last
requirement, the Ghost had appeared to Hamlet in the closet
scene, and for the same reason Hamlet was made to observe
Fortinbras and his army marching across "a plain in Denmark."
For the same reason in this scene Lady Macbeth speaks in such
shockingly violent terms:

> I have given suck, and know
> How tender 'tis to love the babe that milks me.
> I would, while it was smiling in my face,
> Have pluck'd my nipple from his boneless gums
> And dash'd the brains out, had I so sworn as you
> Have done to this.

1. 7. 54-9

So also, to Macbeth's assertion:

> I dare do all that may become a man.
> Who dares do more is none.

which is sound doctrine, implying the notion of decorum and
the mean, Lady Macbeth answers with the old commonplace
that Iago had used, of soul and sense, distinguishing man from
beast through the characteristic of willed action:

> What beast was't then
> That made you break this enterprise to me?
> When you durst do it, then you were a man;
> And to be more than what you were, you would
> Be so much more the man.

1. 7. 46-51

This is obvious sophistry. It makes the will and not reason the distinguishing characteristic of man; it opposes rashness to timidity, excluding from consideration the reasonable mean of right courage. But it takes Macbeth in. His only question now is as to the means: "If we should fail?" Lady Macbeth outlines the way in which the murder can be accomplished and suspicion diverted. As soon as the means are proposed Macbeth assents and the moral choice is complete:

> I am settled and bend up
> Each corporal agent to this terrible feat.
> 1. 7. 79-80

This final decision of the soul, accompanied of course by disordered emotion, persists unaltered through the catastrophe.

But in *Hamlet* the process of moral choice extends throughout the play. The first half is concerned with the choice of end, which rests here as in *Othello* on a question of fact: did Claudius really kill the old King, Hamlet's father? or, what is the same question, is the Ghost a true ghost or a diabolical apparition? To resolve this question of fact Hamlet devises the play scene as an *experimentum crucis*: "If he but blench," Hamlet says in a soliloquy, "I know my course" (2. 2. 625-6). At the close of the play scene, when the King does blench, Hamlet turns to Horatio and says, "I'll take the ghost's word for a thousand pound! Didst perceive?" (3. 2. 297-8). The question of fact is now resolved and Hamlet embraces the end which the Ghost had proposed in an early scene of the play: "Revenge his foul and most unnatural murther" (1. 5. 25). The rest of the play concerns the choice of means, but the means in this case is not easy to find. The King cannot be killed at his prayers and so dispatched to Heaven: "Why, this is hire and salary, not revenge!" (3. 3. 79). He does kill him in the Queen's closet, or so he thinks, but it turns out to be only Polonius, that "wretched, rash, intruding fool." And so on to the close of the play. The proper means to accomplish the

124

end is never discovered until it is too late, until Hamlet when he knows that he is dying stabs the King with the envenomed sword. It is too late, now, for a successful plot.

Hamlet, of course, is a touchy subject. I do not wish to imply that his character is equivalent to this analysis; he is something more and something other. He is an imitation of a person, and thus has an imputed reality. He has a name, which is a chief instrument of individualization. He is implicated in circumstances of some particularity. He does and says much that is not reducible to the central choice. He is presented in a specific body of writing. Nevertheless, a fictional character is not a given, a brute fact of existence. He is a construction, a fiction, and hence he must be constructed according to a scheme and must have a scheme to be intelligible. I am maintaining only that both the play and the character of Hamlet are in part constructed according to the scheme of moral choice as it was analyzed in the scholastic tradition.

It would follow that those who interpret Hamlet's character in terms of irresolution are in a way right, for here the process of choice is extended over the whole play. But they are wrong when they see in this a trait of character. Hamlet delays, not because he is irresolute, but because he is reasonable. His reason must be satisfied as to the end before his will moves to embrace it; his reason must discover the appropriate means before the moral choice can be ratified and action move on to the conclusion. He is irresolute because, as Hooker says, "the Will notwithstanding does not incline to have or do that which Reason teacheth to be good, unless the same do also teach it to be possible" (*EP*, 1. 7. 5). Hamlet could quote in his defense against his detractors, who perhaps like Coleridge are mightier with the pen than with the sword, the apology of the old counsellor in the *Winter's Tale:*

> if ever fearful
> To do a thing where I the issue doubted,
> Whereof the execution did cry out

Against the non-performance, 'twas a fear
That oft infects the wisest.

1. 2. 258-62

Yet in a sense the resolution of the plot is apprehended partly in terms of moral action. Everyone knows the famous line in Hamlet's soliloquy, "Thus conscience," that is, knowledge and awareness, "does make cowards of us all":

And enterprises of great pith and moment
With this regard their current turn awry
And lose the name of action.

3. 1. 83, 86-8

and the later speech prompted by the sight of Fortinbras' exploits:

What is a man,
If his chief good and market of his time
Be but to sleep and feed? A beast, no more.

Here again is the commonplace of soul or sense.

Sure he that made us with such large discourse,
Looking before and after, gave us not
That capability and godlike reason
To fust in us unus'd. Now, whether it be
Bestial oblivion, or some craven scruple
Of thinking too precisely on th' event,—

in which *event,* of course, means "outcome" or "upshot." The problem here involves a choice between no action, rational action with a view to consequences, and action at any cost. The contrast between the latter two resembles that between the chivalric rashness of Hotspur and the staid courage of Prince Hal. In this case it is solved in favor of Hotspur. Hamlet decides:

Rightly to be great
Is not to stir without great argument
But greatly to find quarrel in a straw
When honour's at the stake.

126

and concludes:

> O, from this time forth,
> My thoughts be bloody, or be nothing worth!
>
> 4. 4. 33-41, 53-6, 65-6

From this time forth his actions as well as his thoughts are as bloody as anyone could wish. To the earlier death of Polonius he adds the deaths of Rosencrantz and Guildenstern, of Laertes by accident, and the King by design. He acts now partly from "perfect conscience," in the ethical sense of that which incites or binds us either to do or not to do something, and partly in the rashness of honor. Reasonable action has proved inadequate in the circumstances, and is abandoned:

> Being thus benetted round with villanies,
> Or I could make a prologue to my brains,
> They had begun the play.
>
> 5. 2. 29-31

Deliberation is fatal; only rashness has a chance of success:

> Rashly—
> And prais'd be rashness for it; let us know,
> Our indiscretion sometime serves us well
> When our deep plots do pall; and that should learn us
> There's a divinity that shapes our ends,
> Rough-hew them how we will—
>
> 5. 2. 6-11

Man proposes, and God disposes. Indeed, Heaven is ordinant even in the accidental details. And so Hamlet gives up the human attempt to achieve justice by rational action, by the calculation of means, abandons himself to the tide of circumstance which is the Special Providence of God, and proceeds to the catastrophe despite his misgivings. He is resigned to destiny, which is God's will; "the readiness is all." The play whose plot had displayed the scheme of moral action ends with the renunciation of it.

127

Notes

This book was completed in 1945. I have since cut, rearranged, and rephrased parts of it but have made no substantial alterations. I have cited Shakespeare throughout from *The Complete Works*, ed. George Lyman Kittredge (Boston, 1936). I have generally modernized texts.

I. *Introduction: Ripeness is All*

1. G. B. Harrison, *Shakespeare: 23 Plays and the Sonnets* (New York, 1948), p. 3. Similarly O. J. Campbell, *The Living Shakespeare* (New York, 1949), p. 1: "In his plays we constantly meet our own experiences; in his poetry we constantly find our inmost thoughts and feelings expressed with an eloquence and a precision far beyond our reach."
2. T. S. Eliot, *Selected Essays* (New York, 1932), p. 231.
3. Robert Bechtold Heilman, *This Great Stage* (Baton Rouge, 1948), p. 112. The correct interpretation is given in passing by Alfred Harbage, *As They Liked It* (New York, 1947), p. 56.
4. Hugh Latimer, *Sermons* ("Everyman's Library": London, 1906), pp. 352-3.
5. G. H. Mair, ed. (Oxford, 1909), p. 83.

   John Bruce, ed., Diary of John Manningham ("Camden Society," XCIX: Westminster, 1868), under March 24, 1603: "This morning about three at clock her Majesty departed this life, mildly like a lamb, like a ripe apple from the tree."

II. *Aught of Woe or Wonder*

1. "De ratione studii," *Opera Omnia* (Leyden, 1703), I, 528 C-D. There is a paraphrastic translation of the treatise in William Harrison Woodward, *Desiderius Erasmus concerning the Aim and Method of Education* (Cambridge, 1904), pp. 162-78.
2. *If This be not a Good Play, the Devil is in It* in *Dramatic Works* (Pearson: London, 1873), III, 264.
3. *Opera*, ed. John Burnet (Oxford, 1903), III.

4. *Aristotle on the Art of Poetry*, ed., tr., Ingram Bywater (Oxford, 1909), *ad* 1452a4; 60a11; 60a18.

5. The classic formulation, cited from the index, *s.v.*, *casus*, of the Vives edition (Paris, 1862 and 1861) of Thomas Aquinas, *Summa Theologica*.

6. 2. Prol., 16-7: *The Shakespeare Apocrypha*, ed. C. F. Tucker Brooke (Oxford, 1908), p. 44.

7. "tristitia namque tragoediae proprium." Diomedes *Ars Grammatica* in *Grammatici Latini*, ed. Heinrich Keil (Leipzig, 1857), I, 488.

8. *ST* denotes *Summa Theologica*.

9. Thomas Dekker, "The Magnificent Entertainment . . ." (London, 1604) in *Dramatic Works*, I, 269. Sidney, *Works*, ed. Albert Feuillerat (Cambridge, 1923), III, 23.

10. Hardin Craig, *The Enchanted Glass* (New York, 1936), p. 27; *Shakespeare* (Chicago, 1932), p. 804.

11. *Works*, ed. Keble, 7th ed. (Oxford, 1888). Hereafter referred to as *EP*.

12. However, for a generalized argument see Marston's *Sophonisba*.

13. Julius Caesar Scaliger, *Poetice*, 3. 96; tr., F. M. Padelford, *Select Translations from Scaliger's Poetics* (New York, 1905), p. 57. John Jewel, *The Defense of the Apology* ("Publications of the Parker Society," XXV: Cambridge, 1848), pp. 249-50.

III. *The Donatan Tradition*

1. The material in the following pages is vulgate: Wilhelm Cloetta, *Beiträge zur Literaturgeschichte des Mittelalters und der Renaissance* (Halle, 1890-2); J. E. Spingarn, *A History of Literary Criticism in the Renaissance* (2nd ed., New York, 1908); John W. Cunliffe, ed., *Early English Classical Tragedies* (Oxford, 1912); L. E. Kastner and H. B. Charlton, edd., *The Poetical Works of Sir William Alexander* (Manchester, 1921); A. Philip McMahon, "Seven Questions on Aristotelian·Definitions of Tragedy and Comedy," *Harvard Studies in Classical Philology*, XL (1929), 97-198.

2. "Inter tragoediam autem et comoediam cum multa tum inprimis hoc distat, quod in comoedia mediocres fortunae hominum, parvi impetus periculorum, laetique sunt exitus actionum, at in tragoedia

omnia contra, ingentes personae, magni timores, exitus funesti haben-
tur; et illic prima turbulenta, tranquilla ultima, in tragoedia contrario
ordine res aguntur; tum quod in tragoedia fugienda vita, in comoedia
capessenda exprimitur; postremo quod omnis comoedia de fictis est
argumentis, tragoedia saepe de historia fide petitur." Cited from
McMahon, pp. 128-9. The text is apparently by Evanthius, whose
treatise on comedy is included in the Donatan commentary.
3. A Renaissance commonplace: see Justus Lipsius, *Two Bookes of
Constancie*, tr. Sir John Stradling, ed. Rudolf Kirk (New Brunswick,
N. J., 1939), pp. 85-6.
4. Jacobus Zabarella, *Opera Logica* (Venice, 1586), p. 81: "Quod
Rhetorica et Poetica solius civilis disclipinae instrumenta sint, et
quomodo."
5. *Works*, III, 23.
6. McMahon, *op. cit.*, and "On the Second Book of Aristotle's Poetics
and the Source of Theophrastus' Definition of Tragedy," *Harvard
Studies in Classical Philology*, XXVIII (1917), 1-46.
7. "Tragoedia est heroicae fortunae in adversis conprehensio. a Theo-
phrasto ita definita est, *tragoidia estin eroikes tuches peristasis.* . .
Comoedia est privatae civilisque fortunae sine periculo vitae conprehensio, apud Graecos ita definita, *komoidia estin idiotikon pragmaton
akindunos perioche*. . . in ea viculorum, id est humilium domuum,
fortunae conprehendantur, non ut in tragoedia publicarum regiarum-
que . . . comoedia a tragoedia differt, quod in tragoedia introduc-
untur heroes duces reges, in comoedia humiles atque privatae personae;
in illa luctus exilia caedes, in hac amores, virginum raptus: deinde
quod in illa frequenter et paene semper laetis rebus exitus tristes et
liberorum fortunarumque priorum in peius adgnitio. quare varia
definitione discretae sunt. altera enim *akindunos perioche*, altera
tuches peristasis dicta est. tristitia namque tragoediae proprium."
Keil, *loc. cit.*
8. Cited from Cunliffe, pp. xvi ff.
9. *The Works of Thomas Kyd*, ed. Frederick S. Boas (Oxford, 1901),
p. 164.
10. *The School of Shakespeare*, ed. Richard Simpson (London, 1878),
II, 241ff.
11. *The Shakespeare Apocrypha*, p. 35.

IV. Wonder

1. *Works*, III, 23.

2. For fuller discussion and citation with respect to the history of wonder as an aestheic term see the author's "Tragic Effect and Tragic Process . . . ," unpublished Stanford dissertation, 1945; Richard Heinze, *Virgils Epische Technik* (Leipzig, 1903), pp. 454ff.; Marvin Herrick, "Some Neglected Sources of *Admiratio*," *MLN*. LXII (1947), 222-6. The historians of Renaissance criticism, until Herrick's note, had regarded the concept as introduced in the middle of the sixteenth century by Minturno and without effective influence on the drama until Corneille: Gregory Smith, *Elizabethan Critical Essays* (Oxford, 1904), I, 392; Joel Spingarn, *op. cit.*, 52-3, 72, 78-9, 285; René Bray, *La Formation de la Doctrine Classique en France* (Paris, 1927), 213ff and 319; Allan H. Gilbert, *Literary Criticism: Plato to Dryden* (New York, 1940), 461 and index, *s. v. admiration*.

3. The Bywater translation. For the relationship of wonder *(to thaumaston)* and astonishment *(ekplexis)* see Aristotle, *Topics*, 4. 5. 126b13ff.

4. Gorgias, *Helena*, 9 (ed. Otto Immisch, 1927, though the text seems untrustworthy); E. E. Sikes, *The Greek View of Poetry* (London, 1931); Max Pohlenz, "Die Anfänge der griechischen Poetik," *Nachr. d. Gott. Ges. d. Wiss.*, 1920, pp. 167ff.

5. Tr. Allan H. Gilbert, *op. cit.*, p. 15.

6. Ed. Leonhard Spengel, *Rhetores Graeci* (Leipzig, 1853-6), II, 455.

7. Ed. Émile Bréhier ("Collection Budé": Paris, 1924); translation revised from Stephen McKenna, *The Ethical Treatises* (London, 1926).

8. Ed., tr., Horace Leonard Jones, *The Geography of Strabo* ("Loeb Library": London, 1917).

9. Ed., tr., W. R. Paton, *The Histories* ("Loeb Library": London, 1922).

10. Ed., tr., Frank Cole Babbitt, *Moralia* ("Loeb Library": London, 1927).

11. Cited by Sikes, *op. cit.*, 112.

12. The Oxford translation, as before, but I have revised the second sentence.

13. Cited and translated by G. L. Hendrickson, "The origin and

Meaning of the Ancient Characters of Style," *AJP*, XXVI (1905), 255-6. I have substituted "astonished" for "moved" toward the end of the next to last sentence. Text, Augustus Mayer, ed., *Theophrasti Peri Lexeos Libri Fragmenta* (Leipzig, 1910), pp. 14-5.

14. Tr., T. H. Moxon, *Aristotle's Poetics, Demetrius on Style* (London, 1934); I have made some revisions. Text, W. Rhys Roberts, ed. (Cambridge, 1902).

15. Ed., W. Rhys Roberts (Cambridge, 1907). There is an excellent translation by Benedict Einarson (Chicago, 1945).

16. Ed., H. Rackham ("Loeb Library": London, 1942).

17. Tr., John Selby Watson, *Institutes of Oratory*, 2 vols. (London, 1909-10). I have substituted "wonder" for "admiration" in the last two sentences. Ed., L. Rademacher (Leipzig, 1935).

18. *Patrologia Latina*, XLII, 90.

19. *Opera Omnia*, ed. Augustus Borgnet (Paris, 1890), VI, 30a-31a.

20. My translation.

21. The relevant passages are reprinted and translated by Ruth Kelso, "Girolamo Fracastoro, *Naugerius sive De Poetica Dialogus*," *Univ. of Illinois Studies in Language and Literature*, IX (1924), 75ff.

22. *Ibid.*, pp. 58-9.

23. My translation. The texts are cited in Bernard Weinberg, "The Poetic Theories of Minturno," *Studies in Honor of Frederick W. Shipley* (St. Louis, 1942), pp. 104, n. 6(1), and 110, n. 17.

24. E. K. Chambers, *William Shakespeare* (Oxford, 1930), I, 412 and II, 188.

25. *The Shakespeare Apocrypha.*

26. *The Plays and Poems*, ed. J. Churton Collins (Oxford, 1905).

27. Ed. H. Harvey Wood (Edinburgh, 1934-9).

28. *The Shakespeare Apocrypha.*

29. *Works*, edd. C. H. Herford, Percy and Evelyn Simpson (Oxford, 1925—).

30. *Works*, ed. A. H. Bullen (Boston, 1885-6), VI, 370-1.

V. *Reason Panders Will*

    I am deeply indebted to Lily B. Campbell's *Shakespeare's Tragic Heroes* (Cambridge, 1930), p. 146, for the interpretation of Hamlet's phrase, "reason panders will."

1. "Definitio . . . est imitatio actionis illustris, voluntarie perfectae, cui inest vis universalis circa res praestantiores, non autem particularis

133

de singula re praestanti: qua quidem imitatione animi recta afficiuntur affectione per misericordiam atque terrorem in eis orta." *Voluntarie* can also be construed as an adjective without significant change of meaning. "Paraphrasis in librum Poeticae Aristotelis," tr. Jacobus Mantinus, ed. Fridericus Heidenhain, *Jahrbücher für classische Philologie*, 17th Supplementband (1890), 359. For Renaissance editions see Lane Cooper and Alfred Gudeman, *A Bibliography of the Poetics of Aristotle* ("Cornell Studies in English" XI: New Haven, 1928), *s.n.* Averroes.

2. A medieval commonplace: see Alexander of Hales, *Summa*, 1. 1. 1. ad 1 and ad 2. (Quaracchi, 1924), I.

3. Chas. R. S. Harris, *Duns Scotus* (Oxford, 1927), II, 288ff; see also Arthur C. McGiffert, *History of Christian Thought* (New York, 1932-5), II, 299ff.; D. E. Sharp, *Franciscan Philosophy at Oxford* (Oxford, 1930), pp. 336-41. *ST*, 1-2. 8. 1. For Thomas's doctrine, see Michael Wittmann, *Die Ethik des Hl. Thomas von Aquin* (Munich, 1933); Etienne Gilson, *Moral Values and the Moral Life*, tr. Leo R. Ward (London, 1931).

4. *Phaedra*, 177ff.; *Metamorphoses*, 7. 20-1. These passages are cited by Melanchthon in his refutation of Stoic fatalism, *Corpus Reformatorm* XVI, 42-50, 189-201, and 336-46.

5. *The Enchanted Glass*, 116.

6. Ludwig Schutz, *Thomas-Lexicon* (Paderborn, 1895), *s. vv.*

7. C. F. Tucker Brooke and Nathaniel Burton Paradise, edd., *English Drama: 1580-1642* (Boston, 1933).

8. Ed. A. W. Verity (London, n.d.).

9. The punctuation is from Q1.

10. Ed., G. W. Kitchin ("Everyman's Library": London, 1930), 132.

11. Lancelot Andrewes, *Lectures* (London, 1657), 256.

12. E. E. Stoll, *Othello* (Minneapolis, 1915); *Art and Artifice in Shakespeare* (Cambridge, 1933), p. 6ff.; Hardin Craig, *Shakespeare*, 715-6.

13. John Jewel, *Defence of the Apology*, 70.

14. In the following analysis I obviously owe a good deal to Walter Clyde Curry's *Shakespeare's Philosophical Patterns* (Baton Rouge, 1937).

15. *Advancement of Learning*, p. 146.

16. *The School of Shakespeare*.